Grammar Builder

Level 6
English

Previously published as Success with Grammar series by Scholastic Inc.

This edition published by Scholastic Education International (Singapore) Private Limited
A division of Scholastic Inc.

Scholastic Education International (Singapore) Private Limited
81 Ubi Avenue 4 #02-28 UB.ONE Singapore 408830
education@scholastic.com.sg

First edition 2013

ISBN 978-981-07-5261-3

Welcome to studySMART !

Grammar Builder lets your child review and apply essential grammar rules.

Knowledge of grammar is essential in ensuring your child understands the patterns and rules in the English language. As your child progresses through the practice worksheets, he will strengthen the skills needed to read and write well.

Grammar items covered in one level are reinforced at the subsequent level. This helps to ensure that your child consolidates his learning of a particular grammar item and builds upon it.

Each grammar item is covered in three pages. The first two pages target your child's ability to identify and apply the grammar item. The third page provides a quick assessment of your child's understanding of the use of the grammar item. A revision section at the end of the book also allows for easy assessment of your child's understanding of the grammar items covered in each workbook.

How to use this book?

1. Introduce the target grammar item at the top of the page to your child.

2. Direct your child's attention to the grammar box to review the grammar rule.

3. Let your child complete the practices independently.

4. Use the Assessment pages and Revision section to evaluate your child's understanding of the grammar items.

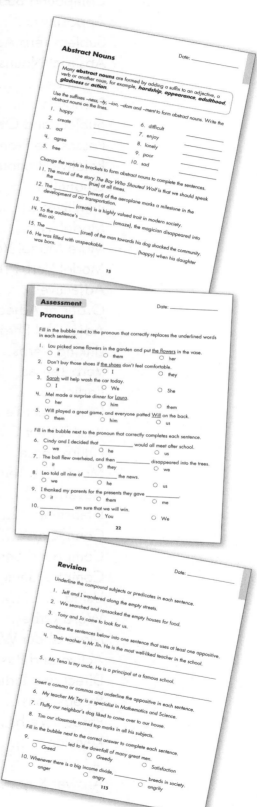

Table of Contents

Compound Subject and Predicate

A **compound subject** is two or more nouns connected by **and** or **or**.
A **compound predicate** is two or more verbs connected by **and** or **or**.

Read the sentences. Underline compound subjects once and compound predicates twice.

1. Annemarie and Ellen are good friends.

2. Their homes and families are in Denmark.

3. The girls sometimes talk or giggle with Annemarie's sister.

4. All three children joke, laugh and play games together.

5. Families and friends help each other in times of need.

6. During the war, the families had to leave their homes and hide their belongings.

7. Annemarie's family hid Ellen and kept her safe.

8. Ellen read and sang to Annemarie's sister, Kirsti.

9. Ellen and Annemarie played with Kirsti.

10. Both the Rosens and the Johansens survived the war.

Select two sentences from above, one with a compound subject and one with a compound predicate. Rewrite each sentence using your own compound subject or predicate.

11. _____

12. _____

Compound Subject and Predicate

Read each pair of sentences. Then, combine them to form a compound subject or a compound predicate. Write the new sentence on the line.

1. Families help each other during times of hardship. Friends help each other during times of hardship.

   _____

2. Many people survive the war with intelligence and courage. Many people survive the war with luck.

   _____

   _____

3. Families hid in the houses. Families fled to the forest.

   _____

4. Sometimes, families were torn apart. Sometimes, they were separated.

   _____

5. Many young people joined the army. Many young people worked in factories.

   _____

6. Many struggled to find food. Many struggled to find drinking water.

   _____

Compound Subject and Predicate

Underline the compound subject or predicate in each sentence.

1. George, Tina and I are playground monitors.

2. We watch for problems and solve them.

3. Keith and Tracy asked me for help with a problem.

4. Their friend, Matt, hit a ball and lost it on the school roof.

5. Tina and I found Matt in a corner of the playground.

6. He showed us where it went and asked if we could help retrieve it.

7. Tina looked up, turned and walked over to Miss Weiss.

8. Miss Weiss told us to find the custodian or find another ball.

Combine each pair of sentences to form a compound subject or a compound predicate.

9. Matt smiled. Matt went to find the custodian.

   _____

10. Miss Weiss waited for Matt to return. I waited for Matt to return.

   _____

Select two sentences from above and rewrite them using your own compound subject or predicate.

11. _____

12. _____

Appositives

An **appositive** is a phrase which comes after a noun or a pronoun. It provides more detail about that noun or pronoun and is always separated from the rest of sentence by a comma or commas. An appositive phrase can be removed without affecting the main idea of the sentence.

Underline the appositive in each sentence.

1. Bananas, my favorite fruit, are part of our dessert this evening.

2. The old lady in the red cardigan, Mrs Briar, lost her purse while shopping at the supermarket.

3. I have to renew my library book, *Animal Farm*, today to avoid late charges.

4. Our cousin, Jayme, will be representing her school in a fencing tournament next month.

5. Mr Cheung, the man with a short beard, helped the police arrest the thief.

Rewrite each sentence without the appositive.

6. Singapore, the country we visited last summer, is a multiracial and multicultural society.

   _____

7. Miss White, my old and tattered toy bunny, is in the wash.

   _____

8. Daniel, the boy with the ponytail, topped my class in Mathematics last year.

   _____

Appositives

Insert commas to indicate the appositive in each sentence.

1. The sun a big ball of burning gas is an important star in our solar system.

2. My sister is trying on a gorgeous wedding gown the one with the beautiful beads in the fitting room.

3. The mischievous boys from Class 6B who had played a prank on their teacher were punished severely by the principal.

4. I saw Josephine my mom's secretary take the stack of documents from the photocopier.

5. Gingerbread Man one of Disney's characters was giving out balloons to children during the parade.

Combine the sentences below into one sentence that uses at least one appositive.

6. Their eldest daughter is Rose. She dislikes being named after a flower.

    _____

7. *The Sunflower* is a beautiful work of art. It was painted by Vincent Van Gogh.

    _____

8. She is Peter's sister. Her name is Martha. She has a new sling bag with a floral print.

    _____

9. Harry Potter has a scar on his forehead. He is a powerful wizard.

    _____

Appositives

Fill in the bubble next to the appositive that correctly completes the sentence.

1. Our neighbors, _____, are from Seattle.
   ○ Bethany and Chris   ○ the man loves cake

2. My favorite festival, _____, is in December.
   ○ I love Christmas   ○ Christmas

3. Jack, _____, was awarded a scholarship for his outstanding academic performance.
   ○ the younger of the twins   ○ he is intelligent

4. Located in the Himalayas is the world's tallest mountain, _____.
   ○ Mount Everest   ○ few have conquered

5. Aunt May served him his favorite food, _____.
   ○ every day   ○ lasagna with meatballs

Insert a comma or commas and underline the appositive in each sentence.

6. A philanthropist Steven Smith donated a huge sum of money to help the victims of the tsunami.

7. Fluffy Grandma's cat loves to purr softly on her lap while she knits in her rocking chair.

8. On Christmas Day, we ate at Zappy our favorite restaurant.

9. Tiffany the most polite student in the class won an award at the school assembly.

10. He was ecstatic when he received his birthday present a new mobile phone.

Subject-Verb Agreement

A singular verb is used with a singular noun or pronoun, an uncountable noun and a collective noun. It is also used with **nobody**, **anybody**, **somebody**, **everybody**, **each**, **every**, **none**, **anyone**, **someone** and **anything**.

Circle the singular noun or pronoun that forms the subject in each sentence. Then, underline the verb it relates to.

1. Dad's car was sent for repairs last Wednesday.

2. Everyone is exhausted after the party; nobody wants to take the trash out.

3. Either of the parents has to attend the parent-teacher conference on Monday.

4. The bunch of bananas that was left on the table last month had become rotten.

5. Hansel is the eldest of the five siblings in the Lee family.

Underline the correct verb to complete each sentence.

6. Air pollution (is / are) becoming a major health hazard in the city.

7. That pair of jade earrings (belong / belongs) to my mother.

8. The security guard (patrol / patrols) the building every hour.

9. The children did not like the salad as the salad cream (was / were) too bland.

10. Aerobics, apart from hiking, (is / are) a good form of exercise.

11. Salt (dissolves / dissolve) faster in hot water than in cold water.

12. (Do / Does) anyone want tomato sauce?

Subject-Verb Agreement

A plural verb is used with a plural noun or pronoun or with a compound subject. When the two nouns connected by **either** ... **or** and **neither** ... **nor** are singular and plural, the verb agrees with the noun closer to it.

Circle the plural noun or pronoun and underline the verb in each sentence.

1. These cookies were sold out quickly because they were freshly baked and delicious.

2. Exercise and a balanced diet keep a man healthy.

3. Neither the pilot nor the passengers were hurt during the emergency landing.

4. My mom and dad are at the movies now.

5. We have taken our dog to the vet for vaccination.

Underline the correct verb to complete each sentence.

6. (Were / Was) you caught in the rain?

7. Mickey Mouse, together with many other Disney characters, (participates / participate) in the parade at Disneyland.

8. All squares (have / has) four equal sides.

9. Some children in the Philippines (scavenge / scavenges) for material, which can be sold or used, from rubbish heaps.

10. Both the helper and my baby sister (has / have) fallen asleep while watching the cartoon.

11. Sand, water and cement (is / are) mixed to make concrete.

12. We (enjoy / enjoys) taking naps on our hammocks after lunch.

Subject-Verb Agreement

Fill in the bubble next to the verb that correctly completes each sentence.

1. The candy boxes, as well as the tangerines, _____ the coming of the Lunar New Year.
   - ○ announce
   - ○ announces

2. The meat _____ become stale after being left outside the whole day.
   - ○ has
   - ○ have

3. Reading _____ to improve one's vocabulary and knowledge.
   - ○ helps
   - ○ help

4. We _____ decided to go to the Maldives for our holiday.
   - ○ has
   - ○ have

5. Nobody _____ playing with a selfish child.
   - ○ enjoys
   - ○ enjoy

6. Every girl _____ to meet her Prince Charming one day.
   - ○ wants
   - ○ want

7. Neither the acting nor the plot of the movie _____ the movie critics.
   - ○ interests
   - ○ interest

8. Both the mobile phone and the computer _____ electronic gadgets that most people cannot do without these days.
   - ○ is
   - ○ are

9. I _____ tired after backpacking for a month.
   - ○ am
   - ○ are

10. Roses, like chocolates, _____ popular Valentine's Day gifts.
    - ○ makes
    - ○ make

Abstract Nouns

> **Abstract nouns** refer to things we cannot touch or see. They usually refer to ideas, concepts and feelings.

Underline the abstract noun in each sentence.

1. The knight had great perseverance and his training paid off.

2. The king commended the knight on his chivalry.

3. The knight also enjoyed great popularity with the people.

4. People admired him for his honesty and integrity.

5. However, to their disappointment, the knight became corrupted.

6. Greed and discontentment have been the downfalls of many great men.

Underline the abstract noun that best completes each sentence.

7. The theme of our staff development day is (unity / childhood).

8. The breathtaking (truth / beauty) of the Grand Canyon draws many visitors to Arizona every year.

9. (Hungry / Hunger) and cold kept the victims of the earthquake awake most of the nights.

10. Many marketing strategies play on man's (vanity / goodness) to sell products.

11. (Jealousy / Fear) among siblings is common in young children.

12. The (emptiness / discovery) of the huge dark hall frightened the child.

Abstract Nouns

> Many **abstract nouns** are formed by adding a suffix to an adjective, a verb or another noun, for example, **hardship**, **appearance**, **adulthood**, **gladness** or **action**.

Use the suffixes *–ness*, *–ty*, *–ion*, *–dom* and *–ment* to form abstract nouns. Write the abstract nouns on the lines.

1. happy   _____
2. create   _____
3. act   _____
4. agree   _____
5. free   _____

6. difficult   _____
7. enjoy   _____
8. lonely   _____
9. poor   _____
10. sad   _____

Change the words in brackets to form abstract nouns to complete the sentences.

11. The moral of the story *The Boy Who Shouted Wolf* is that we should speak the _____ (true) at all times.

12. The _____ (invent) of the aeroplane marks a milestone in the development of air transportation.

13. _____ (create) is a highly valued trait in modern society.

14. To the audience's _____ (amaze), the magician disappeared into thin air.

15. The _____ (cruel) of the man towards his dog shocked the community.

16. He was filled with unspeakable _____ (happy) when his daughter was born.

Abstract Nouns

Fill in the bubble next to the abstract noun that correctly completes
the sentence.

1. During the war, many civilians suffered great _____.
   - ○ gladness   ○ hardship   ○ disgrace

2. His _____ has cost him the opportunity to learn from a great teacher.
   - ○ pride   ○ bravery   ○ proud

3. Abraham Lincoln worked hard to abolish _____.
   - ○ slave   ○ slavery   ○ punishment

4. The smugglers took every _____ to avoid being caught.
   - ○ steps   ○ cautious   ○ precaution

5. The hill fire started due to the _____ of the tomb sweepers.
   - ○ neglecting   ○ neglected   ○ negligence

Form an abstract noun from the underlined word in each sentence. Write the
abstract noun on the line.

6. The students <u>admired</u> their music teacher very much. _____

7. The emperor was <u>just</u> and compassionate. _____

8. It is <u>important</u> to exercise every day. _____

9. Go home quickly. It is <u>dangerous</u> to stay out during a storm. _____

10. All great writers are <u>imaginative</u>. _____

Gerunds

> **Gerunds** are formed by adding **–ing** to verbs. They behave like nouns. Prepositions and articles are often used before gerunds. A **gerund phrase** consists of a group of words starting with a gerund.

Underline the gerund or gerund phrase in each sentence.

1. Gardening is a common hobby in this community.

2. I enjoy swimming and dancing.

3. Toddlers are not adept at controlling their emotions.

4. The persistent ringing of the phone woke me up.

5. Visiting is not permitted beyond certain hours.

6. The chirping of the crickets makes me drowsy.

Read each sentence. Form the correct gerund from the words in brackets.

7. _____ (smoke) is bad for health.

8. She is good at _____ (write) and _____ (act).

9. He was punished severely by his parents for _____ (lie).

10. The two children love _____ (eat)!

11. _____ (steal) was the only way he could think of to survive.

12. _____ (sleep) during class is bound to get you punished.

Gerunds

Identify the gerund in each sentence. Write it on the line.

1. Peter and Chris are fond of jogging every day. _____

2. The couple enjoy traveling during summer. _____

3. Worrying is not going to solve the problem. _____

4. This is what I call a life worth living. _____

5. He started his speech with a personal sharing. _____

Fill in the blank with a gerund formed from the word in brackets.

My grandmother was a big fan of 6. _____ (knit).

She used to knit pullovers and scarves for us for Christmas. She also loved

7. _____ (cook) and she would cook up a storm in the kitchen.

She spent much of her time doing the 8. _____ (wash) and

9. _____ (clean) at home. Sometimes, I would help her with the

10. _____ (iron). As for my grandfather, he spends his time

11. _____ (sing) songs to his pet bird. He likes nothing better than to sit

at home 12. _____ (read) or 13. _____ (sleep).

Date: _____

Gerunds

Fill in the bubble next to the gerund that correctly completes the sentence.

1. Jasmine loves _____; her house is filled with the paintings she has done over the years.
   - ○ painting
   - ○ to paint
   - ○ paintings

2. My mom has an aversion to _____. She refuses to go to places where smoking is not prohibited.
   - ○ smoking
   - ○ to smoke
   - ○ smoked

3. _____ is a big part of my life now, and I aim to take part in the national competition.
   - ○ Skiing
   - ○ Skis
   - ○ Skiers

4. _____ seems to be all the baby does!
   - ○ Cry
   - ○ Crying
   - ○ Cries

5. Instead of working on their projects, the students wasted a lot of time _____.
   - ○ chatted
   - ○ chatting
   - ○ chat

6. He has developed a keen interest in _____.
   - ○ windsurfing
   - ○ windsurf
   - ○ windsurfers

7. You should stop _____ and be grateful instead.
   - ○ complaints
   - ○ complaining
   - ○ complain

8. All I could hear was the _____.
   - ○ scream
   - ○ screams
   - ○ screaming

9. One way of being environmentally conscious is by _____.
   - ○ recycle
   - ○ recycled
   - ○ recycling

10. The man had little time for his family as he spent all his time _____.
    - ○ work
    - ○ worker
    - ○ working

Pronouns

> A **pronoun** is a word that takes the place of a noun or nouns.

Underline the pronouns in each sentence.

1. Eva called Elaine and they agreed to have lunch together.

2. "What time should we meet?" asked Elaine.

3. Eva said that she had classes in the morning.

4. "I think we should meet at noon," said Eva.

5. Elaine said that it was a good time to meet.

Read each sentence pair. Underline the pronouns. On the lines, write the nouns they replace. The first one has been done for you.

6. Joe bought a gift last week. He gave it to Margaret yesterday.

    _____He = Joe_____   _____it = gift_____

7. Many people are in line, waiting to buy the book. They have been waiting to buy it all afternoon.

    _____   _____

8. Amy and Duncan paddled for three hours. "We have been paddling all afternoon," said Amy, "and I am getting tired."

    _____   _____

9. Did Emma get the eggs? She will need them for dinner.

    _____   _____

10. Timmy found his shoes. He was looking for them all day.

    _____   _____

Pronouns

Read the sentences. Write a pronoun on the line that can replace the underlined words.

1. <u>Talent shows</u> can make people nervous. _____

2. <u>A talent show</u> gives people a chance to show off. _____

3. <u>My brother</u> was in the school talent show. _____

4. <u>Lots of people</u> clapped for my brother. _____

5. <u>My sister</u> did not want to be in the show. _____

6. I can't blame <u>my sister</u> for feeling that way. _____

7. I was nervous about being in <u>the talent show</u>, too. _____

8. <u>Pam, Alicia and I</u> decided to sing a round. _____

9. People clapped politely for <u>Pam, Alicia and me</u>. _____

10. We thanked <u>the audience</u> for applauding. _____

11. You can ask <u>Mrs Renko</u> about how well we did. _____

Imagine that you are dancing or singing in a talent show and the music suddenly stops. Write three sentences telling how you feel and how others react. Underline all the pronouns that you use.

12. _____

13. _____

14. _____

Pronouns

Fill in the bubble next to the pronoun that correctly replaces the underlined words in each sentence.

1. Lou picked some flowers in the garden and put <u>the flowers</u> in the vase.
   ○ it   ○ them   ○ her

2. Don't buy those shoes if <u>the shoes</u> don't feel comfortable.
   ○ it   ○ I   ○ they

3. <u>Sarah</u> will help wash the car today.
   ○ I   ○ We   ○ She

4. Mel made a surprise dinner for <u>Laura</u>.
   ○ her   ○ him   ○ them

5. Will played a great game, and everyone patted <u>Will</u> on the back.
   ○ them   ○ him   ○ us

Fill in the bubble next to the pronoun that correctly completes each sentence.

6. Cindy and I decided that _____ would all meet after school.
   ○ we   ○ he   ○ us

7. The ball flew overhead, and then _____ disappeared into the trees.
   ○ it   ○ they   ○ we

8. Leo told all nine of _____ the news.
   ○ we   ○ he   ○ us

9. I thanked my parents for the presents they gave _____.
   ○ it   ○ them   ○ me

10. _____ am sure that we will win.
    ○ I   ○ You   ○ We

Subject and Object Pronouns

> A **subject pronoun** takes the place of a noun or nouns as the subject of a sentence. Words, such as **I**, **you**, **she**, **he**, **it**, **we** and **they**, are subject pronouns. An **object pronoun** takes the place of a noun or nouns as the object of a sentence. Words, such as **me**, **you**, **him**, **her**, **it**, **us** and **them**, are object pronouns.

Read the sentence pairs below. Underline the pronoun in the second sentence. Then, circle the noun it replaces in the first sentence.

1. The woodcutter saw a neighbor in the garden. The woodcutter approached him.

2. "Those roses are beautiful," said the woodcutter. "They have a wonderful scent."

3. "This garden is a joy," said the neighbor. "It gets a lot of sun."

4. "There's an easier way to dig holes," said the woodcutter. "A shovel could dig them in half the time."

5. The neighbor just smiled at the woodcutter and said, "Good day to you, sir."

Underline the pronouns in the sentences below. Above each one, write *S* if it is a subject pronoun and *O* if it is an object pronoun.

6. The woodcutter's wife asked him to go to the woods.

7. "I want you to chop some wood," she said.

8. "We have guests coming to visit us," said the woodcutter's wife.

9. "They will be here soon. Let's serve them dinner," she said.

10. The woodcutter found an ax and he picked it up.

11. "I will be back soon," the woodcutter told her.

Date: _____

Subject and Object Pronouns

Circle the correct pronoun to complete each sentence.

1. Mr Todd's wife warns (he / him) to be careful while driving.

2. He ignores (she / her) and does not listen.

3. In fact, he seldom listens to (she / her).

4. (They / Them) just don't see eye to eye on many things.

5. Amy and (I / me) feel sorry for Mr Todd.

6. (He / Him) does not seem like such an unlikeable character.

7. (We / Us) sometimes ignore advice as well.

8. We told Katie about Mr and Mrs Todd and (she / her) had a different opinion.

9. (Her / She) opinion is that Mr Todd was in the wrong.

10. (He / Him) should listen to his wife.

Write four sentences telling how you feel or react when people give you advice. Use as many subject and object pronouns as possible.

11. _____

12. _____

13. _____

14. _____

Date: _____

Subject and Object Pronouns

Fill in the bubble next to the pronoun that correctly completes each sentence.

1. _____ will all meet at my house after the game.
   ○ We   ○ Them   ○ Us

2. _____ decided to hold the meeting tomorrow after school.
   ○ They   ○ Them   ○ Us

3. Lydia and _____ are going to be in the play.
   ○ me   ○ I   ○ us

4. Bruce met _____ at the football game.
   ○ me   ○ I   ○ we

5. Jeff bought a used bike and painted _____ red.
   ○ it   ○ him   ○ them

Decide if the underlined part of each sentence is correct. Fill in the bubble next the right answer.

6. <u>They</u> tried out for the basketball team.
   ○ Them   ○ Us   ○ correct as is

7. Susan promised to take <u>they</u> to the lake tomorrow.
   ○ them   ○ we   ○ correct as is

8. Dad took <u>I and Mark</u> to the beach today.
   ○ Mark and I   ○ Mark and me   ○ correct as is

9. <u>Her and me</u> have been friends for a long time.
   ○ Me and she   ○ She and I   ○ correct as is

10. <u>Me and him</u> are exactly the same age.
    ○ Him and me   ○ He and I   ○ correct as is

Possessive Forms

> We use **possessive pronouns**, like *mine*, *yours*, *his*, *hers*, *ours* and *theirs*, to show ownership or belonging. We also use **possessive adjectives**, like *my*, *your*, *his*, *her*, *its*, *our* and *their*, to show ownership.

Circle the possessive pronoun or adjective in each sentence. Write the noun it relates to on the line.

1. My family is moving next summer, so we're packing all the things that belong to us.   _____

2. You won't believe what we found in our attic.   _____

3. Mom and Dad found a stack of old photos from their honeymoon.   _____

4. Ella found her first bicycle.   _____

5. Adam found his diary.   _____

6. Now, he is looking for its key.   _____

7. What do you think you would find in your house?   _____

Write the possessive pronoun that goes with each subject pronoun.

8. I _____   12. it _____

9. you _____   13. we _____

10. he _____   14. they _____

11. she _____

Possessive Forms

Circle the correct possessive pronoun or adjective to complete each sentence.

1. They practiced (their / theirs) lines over and over again.

2. She uses (her / hers) talent to create beautiful paintings.

3. "Is that (my / mine) playbook?" asked Lily.

4. "No, it is (my / mine)," replied Sean.

5. The play is about a woman's struggle to find (her / hers) missing sister.

Rewrite the sentences, using a suitable possessive form in place of the underlined words.

6. Which dresses in the closet are Barbara's?

    _____

7. This is Ken and Tony's collection of dried flowers.

    _____

8. I am enjoying Paul's book.

    _____

9. Elizabeth's disappointment showed clearly.

    _____

10. Is this Kevin's idea?

    _____

Date: _____

Possessive Forms

Fill in the bubble next to the possessive form that correctly completes each sentence.

1. Every night, the older children on _____ block get together.
   ○ mine   ○ my   ○ ours

2. If Lila is there, we play basketball at _____ house.
   ○ her   ○ hers   ○ its

3. When Ray and Maria are home, we play at _____.
   ○ its   ○ theirs   ○ their

4. Tonight, Al and Rob are bringing _____ soccer ball.
   ○ his   ○ theirs   ○ their

5. Tomorrow night, I will bring _____.
   ○ mine   ○ my   ○ our

Decide which possessive pronoun replaces the underlined words. Fill in the bubble next to the correct answer.

6. <u>Mr and Mrs Es's</u> daughter Tracy won a trophy for soccer.
   ○ Theirs   ○ Their   ○ Her

7. This year's most valuable player's name is written on <u>the trophy's</u> base.
   ○ my   ○ its   ○ her

8. <u>Tracy's</u> team will play in the competition.
   ○ Our   ○ Her   ○ Hers

9. Last year, <u>Alan's</u> school won the championship.
   ○ him   ○ his   ○ its

10. This year, victory will be <u>Tracy's</u>.
   ○ her   ○ theirs   ○ hers

Relative Pronouns

A **relative pronoun** gives more information about the noun in the independent clause. The most common relative pronouns are **who**, **whom**, **which**, **whose** and **that**. **Who** and **whom** are used for people, **whose** is used to show possession, **which** is used for animals and things, and **that** is used for people, animals and things.

Circle the relative pronoun in each sentence.

1. The tall, thin man, who came to Grandpa's house last Saturday, is my uncle from Vancouver.

2. Is there anyone on whom we can depend in times of difficulty?

3. The boy whose toy train broke wailed loudly in the restaurant.

4. The comic book that you lent me yesterday was funny and interesting.

5. My sister, who is an elementary school teacher, loves to sing and paint.

Read each sentence. Circle the relative pronoun and underline the noun it refers to.

6. Students who work hard throughout the year usually do well during assessments.

7. This is the shop that sells the DVD you are looking for.

8. Children who bully others usually have low self-esteem.

9. The man whose house was broken into was very sad.

10. The bus, which leaves at seven o'clock, goes directly to my school.

11. The pretty girl, who is playing the clarinet, is her youngest daughter.

Relative Pronouns

Fill in the blank with a suitable relative pronoun.

1. The dump truck, _____ is a huge machine, could carry all the debris to the landfill in a single trip.

2. The reckless driver, _____ knocked into the poor old lady, was sentenced to six months imprisonment.

3. The guest speaker, _____ is scheduled to speak at today's seminar, has fallen ill.

4. You must return this valuable diamond necklace to _____ it belongs.

5. Deon, _____ father is a firefighter, is determined to follow in his footsteps.

Complete the sentences using the relative pronoun provided.

6. Annie told me about the teacher whom _____
   _____.

7. The gardener trapped the rabbit that _____
   _____.

8. Tarantulas, which _____, have eight legs.

9. Mrs Wright put on the red evening gown that _____
   _____.

10. Jonathan, whose _____, is walking up to us now.

11. Joanna dislikes the classmate who _____.

Date: _____

Relative Pronouns

Fill in the bubble next to the relative pronoun that correctly completes the sentence.

1. Why did you take the diamond earrings _____ do not belong to you?
   ○ who   ○ whose   ○ that

2. Clearance sales, _____ happen at the end of each season, are a great way to save money.
   ○ who   ○ which   ○ whom

3. The man _____ computer crashed could not complete his report.
   ○ whom   ○ whose   ○ who

4. This is the dog _____ was abandoned by its owner.
   ○ who   ○ whom   ○ that

5. The teacher _____ retired last month was adored by all her students.
   ○ who   ○ whose   ○ that

Join the two sentences using a suitable relative pronoun.

6. The adorable baby is sleeping in the room. She is my niece.

   _____

7. The fisherman's boat capsized due to the storm. He is safe.

   _____

8. These are the carnations. I bought them for my mother's birthday.

   _____

Quantifiers

A **quantifier** shows the amount or number of things. They can be used with both countable and uncountable nouns. Look at the table below.

with countable nouns	a few, many, several, a number of, a majority of, both, every, each
with uncountable nouns	much, a little, a bit of, a great deal of, a large amount of, a large quantity of
with both countable and uncountable nouns	all, enough, more/most, less/least, no/none, some, any, a lot of, plenty of, both

Underline the quantifier in each sentence.

1. Mom added a lot of maple syrup to our pancakes.

2. Much of what he said was so ludicrous that even the children did not believe him.

3. The student ushers will each wear a yellow ribbon on his coat.

4. None of the boys likes to eat vegetables.

5. Many people were at the beach today.

6. Can you pass me some salt, please? The dish is too bland.

7. Mom hurried to the supermarket to buy milk for the baby as there isn't any left.

8. The Lees left for the airport a few hours ago.

9. Most of the strawberries have gone bad.

10. Every driver has to pass a written examination on traffic rules before learning to drive.

11. Matthew ate some of the sandwiches we packed for the picnic.

12. All the village boys will have to go through the rite of passage when they are thirteen.

Quantifiers

Put a tick in the brackets if the underlined quantifier shows the quantity of a countable noun and a cross if it shows the quantity of an uncountable noun.

1. (   ) Please carry <u>a few</u> recyclable bags because we are going grocery shopping.

2. (   ) He put <u>all</u> the blame on his classmates when the project was not completed in time.

3. (   ) Do you have <u>any</u> tomato sauce to go with the chips?

4. (   ) <u>Both</u> the boys love playing with toy cars.

5. (   ) How many <u>fewer</u> buses are there than cars on the road?

6. (   ) There is <u>a lot of</u> laughter at home whenever Uncle Ronald is in town.

Fill in each blank with a suitable quantifier from the box. Use each quantifier once only.

little	a lot of	much	some	any	many

7. There is very _____ hot water left in the thermal flask; we need to boil more.

8. The man was starving, so he ate _____ bowls of rice.

9. Please do not put _____ sugar in my coffee.

10. There was _____ noise at the construction site.

11. Here are _____ of his paintings; they are loud and colorful.

12. There is not _____ information on the missing child.

Quantifiers

Fill in the bubble next to the quantifier that best completes each sentence.

1. There is _____ of food for everyone at the buffet.
   - ○ many
   - ○ plenty
   - ○ few

2. You need not bring so _____ books to school.
   - ○ many
   - ○ plenty
   - ○ much

3. I have _____ money in my wallet.
   - ○ a few
   - ○ little
   - ○ many

4. Sarah collected a large _____ of shells from the beach.
   - ○ amount
   - ○ number
   - ○ many

5. I do not have as _____ hair clips as my sister.
   - ○ many
   - ○ much
   - ○ little

Fill in the blank with a suitable quantifier from the box. Use each quantifier once only.

lots of	much	few	a little	many

6. How _____ would the teddy bear cost?

7. _____ students know as much about the solar system as Ian.

8. She has so _____ dresses that she cannot decide which one to wear to the party.

9. The builders need to drink _____ water.

10. There is only _____ milk left in the carton.

Infinitives

> The **infinitive** is the base form of a verb. It is always in the simple present tense. The infinitive with **to** is used after a noun, a pronoun or a verb to express purpose. The infinitive without **to** is used after modal verbs such as **may**, **must** and **can**. It is also used after verbs such as **see**, **let** and **make**.

Underline the infinitive in each sentence.

1. The children might go to Disneyland tomorrow.

2. My brother wanted to accompany his friend to the mall.

3. The young couple plans to buy a house when they have saved up enough money.

4. The dog is too weak to walk after not having eaten for three days.

5. I let my pet dog run around the park.

6. I let him stay the night because of the fierce typhoon.

Read each sentence. Underline the correct form of the verb in brackets.

7. He learnt to (ride / rides / rode) a horse at the age of six.

8. Sophie can (sing / sings / singing) so well that even passersby stop to listen.

9. Luckily it started to (rain / rains / raining) only after we got back home.

10. We saw a monkey trying to (escape / escaped / escaping) from its cage while the zookeeper was feeding the other monkeys.

11. She picked some sea shells at the beach to (decorate / decorating / decorated) the photo frame.

Infinitives

Underline the correct infinitive in brackets to complete each sentence.

1. They went to (watch / tell) the musical, *Cats,* when they were in London.

2. She began to (tidy / brush) up the room when she saw the mess the children made after their art class.

3. The policeman told the man he could (clean / leave) the police station after taking his statement.

4. It takes hard work and perseverance to (toil / succeed) in life.

5. Despite being sick for a week, Adam refused to (see / watch) a doctor.

6. Daphne and Chris decided to (sell / paint) their house as they were moving to another country.

Complete the sentences with suitable infinitives.

7. He was reluctant to _____.

8. You may _____if you please.

9. I am excited _____.

10. A camel can _____for a long period of time.

11. He ran as fast as he could _____.

12. Crystal bought a new dress _____.

Assessment

Infinitives

Fill in the bubble next to the infinitive to correctly complete the sentence.

1. We saw him _____ across the road even though the traffic light had turned red.
   - ○ dash
   - ○ dashed
   - ○ to dash

2. The young boy refused to _____ crying despite all his parents' attempts to please him.
   - ○ begin
   - ○ stop
   - ○ commence

3. She struggled to _____ her children after her husband left home suddenly.
   - ○ visit
   - ○ raise
   - ○ fed

4. Here is a box to _____ your lunch in.
   - ○ puts
   - ○ putting
   - ○ put

5. A chameleon can _____ its color to escape danger.
   - ○ change
   - ○ changing
   - ○ changed

Complete the sentence using a suitable infinitive.

6. We asked him to _____.

7. The teacher demanded _____.

8. You must _____.

9. She let me _____.

10. The chef's recipe is too difficult _____

    _____.

Modal Verbs

A **modal verb** is a verb that can express likelihood, ability, permission or obligation. It can also give advice. Look at the table below.

can / could	ability
must	probability / necessity
should / ought to	advice
can / could / may	ask for / give permission
will / would	habits, things we usually do or did in the past / invitation / request / futurity
might	possibility

Underline the correct modal verb to complete each sentence.

1. Mr Wong (could / may) go to the dentist tomorrow if his tooth hurts.

2. You (can / might) pack you school bag and go home.

3. He (may / could) run as fast as a horse when he was younger.

4. Dorothy (can / might) sing well and is part of our school choir.

5. After fasting for two days, they (could / must) be very hungry.

6. Please get your umbrellas ready as it (must / may) rain later.

Fill in the blanks with *can, could, may* or *might*.

7. Mom is excited that my little brother _____ count to twenty.

8. If he goes for early treatment, he _____ not have to undergo the operation.

9. The girls had a busy day at school, so they _____ not want to go to the movies tonight.

10. How _____ you be so careless? You could have hurt yourself!

11. Gavin said he _____ bake a cake if had time during the day.

Modal Verbs

Underline the modal verb that best completes each sentence.

1. To keep the beach clean, we (should / may) dispose of our trash properly.

2. This song (could / ought to) win the award this year.

3. "You (shall / may) pay for this," yelled the owner of the damaged car.

4. You (can / must) study hard if you want to do well in your test.

5. The boys (will / could) apologize to their neighbor tomorrow for breaking his window.

6. I (shall / ought to) report you to the police for stealing.

Fill in the blanks with *shall, will, must, ought to* or *should.*

7. If you do not study hard, you _____ not be able to score well.

8. You _____ not quit school at such a young age; if you do so, you will not be able to get a good job.

9. Priscilla promised that she _____ come to my party next week.

10. We _____ put on masks when we are sick so that we do not pass the germs to others.

11. I_____ not get angry so easily and be more understanding.

12. We _____ be filial to our parents and take care of them when they grow old.

Modal Verbs

Fill in the bubble next to the modal verb that best completes each sentence.

1. Do not go near the rat; it _____ bite!
   ○ ought to   ○ may   ○ should

2. I _____ wake up early tomorrow so that I can join them for a swim before work.
   ○ can   ○ shall   ○ might

3. You _____ get well soon so that you can take part in the competition.
   ○ can   ○ will   ○ must

4. My uncle had been traveling for two weeks. He _____ be exhausted!
   ○ can   ○ will   ○ should

5. Abby is a linguist; she _____ speak seven languages.
   ○ can   ○ will   ○ should

Underline the modal verb and decide if it indicates ability (A), intention (I) or obligation (O). Write the letter on the line.

6. Everyone in the family knows that I can type faster than my sister.
   _____

7. She will wear the blue gown to the prom. _____

8. As citizens, we must vote for people who are capable of governing our country justly. _____

9. He could dazzle the female audiences with his charming smile when he was in his twenties. _____

10. I must return my library books tomorrow to avoid paying the fine.
   _____

More Modal Verbs

The modal verb **need** is used to convey a duty, necessity or an obligation. The modal verb **dare** is used in negative and interrogative statements to express being brave enough, strong disapproval or outrage.

Underline the modal verb in each sentence. Decide if it expresses necessity (N), bravery (B) or outrage (O). Write the letter on the line.

1. We need to give our best to everything we do. _____

2. Fearing that the serpent would know he was hiding behind the sculpture, Harry Potter dared not move under his invisible cloak. _____

3. Don't you dare yell at the old woman! She was just trying to help. _____

4. Do I need to go to the supermarket? _____

5. It was pitch dark outside, so Kyle dared not open his eyes. _____

Fill in the blanks with *need* or *dare*.

6. You _____ to have enough rest, otherwise you won't recover.

7. The smugglers _____ not talk loudly in case the passengers on the deck heard them.

8. I _____ to add more sugar to my cheesecake as it is not sweet enough.

9. _____ you leave the class now? We have just begun the lesson.

10. Rhonda did not _____ disobey her mother as she did not want to be grounded.

More Modal Verbs

Fill in the blanks with appropriate modal verbs.

1. We _____ be able to finish our project if we follow the schedule given closely.

2. _____ you pass me the salt and pepper, please?

3. He has never been late; he _____ be caught in a traffic jam.

4. I _____ you to jump into the fast-moving river, since you claimed to be such an excellent swimmer.

5. Josephine _____ punch her life-sized teddy bear whenever she is furious.

6. Abraham _____ apologize to Grandma for breaking her favorite vase.

Complete the sentences using suitable modal verbs.

7. The surgeons _____; the operation has lasted for nine hours!

8. She is so fierce, _____.

9. You _____, you could have been killed!

10. Mrs Wong _____, otherwise she will have to pay a huge amount of interest.

11. The board is so dirty. Justin, _____?

More Modal Verbs

Fill in the bubble next to the correct modal verb.

1. James' mother suspected that James _____ have speech delay as he only uttered his first word at the age of four.
    - ○ might   ○ ought to   ○ should

2. I shall complete my homework quickly so that I _____ cycle with my neighbors.
    - ○ can   ○ shall   ○ dare

3. I _____ to be hospitalized so that I can have an X-ray done on my injured leg.
    - ○ will   ○ need   ○ dare

4. He did not _____ to ask the popular girl to the dance.
    - ○ must   ○ should   ○ dare

5. Do you _____ to enter that eerie-looking house?
    - ○ can   ○ need   ○ dare

Fill in the blanks with *dare, need, can, will* or *should*. Use each word once only.

6. All the children _____ know the letters of the alphabet by the time they are in year one.

7. Do you _____ approach the stranger for directions?

8. We _____ to put the potted plant in a bright and airy place so that it grows well.

9. The acrobats _____ check their equipment again just before the show commences.

10. All the students are impressed that Mrs Wright _____ write and draw so beautifully with both hands.

Modal Verbs That Talk about Habit

The **modal verbs *will*, *would*** and ***used to*** are used to convey habits. ***Used to*** and ***would*** are used to express past habits. ***Used to*** can also be used to convey past state. ***Will*** is used to express present habit.

Underline the modal verb in each sentence. Write *present* if it expresses a present habit and *past* if it expresses a past habit.

1. She will glance in a funny way whenever her mother is mentioned. _____

2. When we were young, Mom used to tell us bedtime stories. _____

3. He would hum whenever he was happy. _____

4. Every Sunday, we will go for a walk in the park. _____

5. Dad used to sleep in late on Sundays, but now he wakes up early to take the dog for a walk. _____

Fill in the blanks with *would* or *used to*.

I 6. _____ live in a small town by the beach. Mom was a

school teacher then. She 7. _____ teach in the town school and

8. _____ come home late in the afternoon. After preparing dinner, she

9. _____ bring my brother and me for a stroll along the sandy, white

beach. I 10. _____ watch the fishing boats come in after a day's catch.

The seagulls 11. _____ hover above the sea, waiting eagerly for

their dinner.

Modal Verbs That Talk about Habit

Fill in the blanks with *will, would* or *used to.*

1. On Saturdays, after her ballet classes, she _____ come home exhausted.

2. Every day, I _____ drink a glass of fruit juice after lunch.

3. The dog _____ wag its tail fervently whenever it sees its owner.

4. In their younger days, the boys _____ show off their manliness.

5. He _____ hate writing, but now he is a famous journalist.

6. When the children were living with me, they _____ help me mow the lawn every week.

7. She _____ come home whenever she has a school break.

Complete the sentences using *used to, would* or *will.*

8. When I was young, _____.

9. Every morning, Grandpa _____.

10. He _____,
    but he doesn't do it anymore.

11. They _____
    when they were living in Paris.

12. Whenever Mom is on a business trip, Dad _____

    _____.

Modal Verbs That Talk about Habit

Fill in the bubble next to the modal verb that best completes each sentence.

1. Uncle Greg, my mother's brother, _____ carry me on his back whenever he visited us.
   ○ will   ○ would   ○ should

2. Every afternoon, Grandma _____ watch her favorite drama serial till Grandpa returns home.
   ○ will   ○ used to   ○ could

3. When we were living in Japan, Aunt Carol _____ bring us to Disneyland every Christmas.
   ○ will   ○ dare   ○ would

4. My cousin _____ practice law, but now he is studying medicine.
   ○ must   ○ used to   ○ should

5. Mrs Burrell _____ be a full-time housewife until Mr Burrell passed away a year ago.
   ○ need   ○ used to   ○ ought to

Fill in the blanks with suitable modal verbs from the box. Use each word once only.

will	must	can	would	should

6. Unlike human beings, fish _____ live in the water.

7. We _____ play chess every evening when we were young.

8. You _____ notify the school if you cannot attend classes.

9. The owner of the hotel _____ have it cleaned every year before the peak period.

10. Plants _____ have sunlight, water and air to survive.

Adjectives

> **Adjectives** describe nouns. They tell more about a person, place or thing.

Underline the adjective(s) in each sentence.

1. The hungry, black dog ate up my sausage bun.

2. The friendly pilot gave my brother a short tour of the cockpit after the plane landed at the airport.

3. We used to like watching horror movies with Grandpa.

4. Betsy is the most responsible student in my class; she has never forgotten her homework.

5. The beautiful butterfly fluttered its colorful wings vigorously in its attempt to escape from the glass bottle.

6. Do you know the quickest way to get to the hospital?

7. The gingerbread men looked so adorable and tasted so delicious that they were sold out within two hours.

8. The world's oldest, active passenger ship, *Doulos*, will dock in Hong Kong next month.

Circle the most suitable adjective to complete each sentence.

9. She curls her hair every night as it is long and (straight / curly).

10. I had a big surprise from an (unexpected / regular) visitor today.

11. It will be (difficult / lazy) to farm on such rocky land.

12. With a new coat of paint, the old car looks as good as (new / dull).

13. This book is so (interesting / dull) that Joe couldn't put it down.

Adjectives

Use a suitable suffix from the box to form an adjective with each word below.

–able	–ous	–ful	–ing	–ive

1. teach   _____
2. courage   _____
3. faith   _____
4. adore   _____
5. bore   _____

6. attract   _____
7. help   _____
8. interest   _____
9. fame   _____
10. excite   _____

Fill in the blanks with suitable adjectives.

11. My neighbor is so _____; she offers to babysit for me while I go for dinner with my friends.

12. To make a _____ cup of Chinese tea, you need a _____ teacup and very _____ water.

13. The _____Statue of Liberty is a _____ gift from the French to the Americans.

14. The _____ driver kept changing lanes to get ahead of other drivers.

15. The _____ lord lived in a _____ castle close to the homes of the starving peasants in his estate.

Adjectives

Fill in the bubble next to the adjective that best completes each sentence.

1. This digital camera is too _____ for me to buy for my son.
   ○ expensive   ○ careful   ○ boring

2. We are _____ enough to take care of ourselves.
   ○ lazy   ○ diligent   ○ independent

3. The scientist discovered an _____ source of natural energy that could replace fossil fuel.
   ○ invaluable   ○ impossible   ○ impeccable

4. The dog was _____ and growled at everyone who passed by.
   ○ fierce   ○ timid   ○ fiercely

5. The mountain is too _____ for young children to hike.
   ○ gentle   ○ steep   ○ steeply

Fill in the blanks with suitable adjectives from the box.

| greedy | worried | painful | kind | bitter |

6. The _____ boy ate so many sweets that he developed a stomachache.

7. His mother is _____ that he would also get a toothache.

8. The boy crouched in one corner as it was very _____.

9. The _____ doctor spoke to him gently but sternly.

10. He gave the boy some _____ medicine to take for his pain.

Order of Adjectives

Sometimes, two or more **adjectives** come before a noun to tell more about it. We need to arrange them in a certain order: quality – size – age – shape – color – type.

Underline the adjectives and circle the nouns they describe.

1. The proud Chinese man sells all sorts of things.

2. Mom bought a pretty porcelain tea set for Grandma from him.

3. The man wrapped it up for her in a flowery red wrapping paper.

4. A skinny young lady walked into the shop and wanted to buy the same tea set, but there were none left.

5. Eventually, she bought a soft blue Oriental pillow.

Sort the adjectives according to their types and put them in the correct columns.

Chinese	cotton	blue	young
gigantic	useful	triangular	yellow
silly	metal	sleeping	tiny
round	African	old	strong
plastic	American	tall	brown

Adjectives							
Opinion	**Size**	**Age**	**Shape**	**Color**	**Origin**	**Material**	**Purpose**

Order of Adjectives

Choose the correct order of adjectives by putting a ✓ in the brackets.

1. (   ) an old plastic table
    (   ) a plastic old table
    (   ) a table old plastic

2. (   ) a beautiful colonial white house
    (   ) a colonial beautiful white house
    (   ) a beautiful white colonial house

3. (   ) a serving pretty glass bowl
    (   ) a pretty glass serving bowl
    (   ) a glass pretty serving bowl

4. (   ) a tiny cute brown mongrel
    (   ) a cute tiny brown mongrel
    (   ) a cute brown tiny mongrel

5. (   ) pink socks cotton
    (   ) cotton pink socks
    (   ) pink cotton socks

Complete the sentences by writing the adjectives, given in brackets, in the correct order on the blanks.

6. The girl wearing a _____ dress is my niece. (short, yellow)

7. My _____ lecturer could talk for hours nonstop. (History, boring, old)

8. The British scientist has discovered an _____ cure for Alzheimer's disease. (amazing, new)

9. The _____ chair in the corner of the living room is Grandpa's favorite. (leather, comfortable, old)

10. The _____ lady walking towards us now is very popular in school. (young, intelligent)

Date: _____

Order of Adjectives

Fill in the bubble next to the correct order of adjectives to complete each sentence.

1. Uncle Ken has an _____ dog.
    ○ ugly big black   ○ black big ugly

2. I am going to wear my _____ nose to the Halloween party this evening.
    ○ scary long pointed   ○ long pointed scary

3. This farm produces _____ products such as cheese and yogurt.
    ○ excellent dairy   ○ dairy excellent

4. Mom packed the cupcakes in a _____ box.
    ○ white round recyclable   ○ round white recyclable

5. Please do not discard the _____ bottles on the table; they can be reused.
    ○ empty glass   ○ glass empty

Write the adjectives, given in brackets, in the correct order on the line.

6. (round, reading, tiny)   a _____ lamp

7. (popular, slim, German)   a _____ model

8. (pink, fragile, porcelain, flower) the _____ vase

9. (tall, Science, eccentric)   my _____ teacher

10. (old, haunted, mysterious)   the _____ house

Adjectival Phrases

> An **adjectival phrase** is a group of words that describes a noun.

Underline the adjectival phrase in each sentence.

1. Halloween was a night full of horror for the young boy.

2. The photographs in the album were taken by Grandpa when he was a young man.

3. The forest next to the cottage is dark and eerie.

4. The mysterious room in the attic has been locked for years; no wonder the children are curious to find out what is inside.

5. The animals in this special zoo belong to endangered species and are closely monitored by the World Wildlife Fund.

Tick the sentence with an adjectival phrase.

6. (   ) Grandma used to live in a wooden house.
   (   ) Grandma used to live in a house built of wood.

7. (   ) The baby in the stroller is crying furiously because he is cold and wet.
   (   ) The baby is crying furiously in the stroller because he is cold and wet.

8. (   ) My great grand uncle was a man of great wealth; he owned acres of land.
   (   ) My great grand uncle was a wealthy man; he owned acres of land.

9. (   ) Tigers with white fur tend to be bigger at birth.
   (   ) White tigers tend to be bigger at birth.

10. (   ) Mr Hyde led a decadent life.
    (   ) Mr Hyde led a life of decadence.

Date: _____

Adjectival Phrases

Join each pair of sentences using an adjectival phrase.

1. The girl is mischievous. She is in detention class.

   _____

2. The box is under the bed. It is covered with cobwebs.

   _____

3. The lawn is full of tall weeds. The lawn is between the two old houses.

   _____

4. This is our pet cat, Dolly. It is with the veterinarian.

   _____

5. Did you see the man? He is leaving the car park.

   _____

Fill in the blanks with suitable adjectival phrases.

6. The high-tea buffet _____ is delicious and affordable.

7. The bread _____ has long expired; it is stale and mouldy.

8. The emperor wore a gown _____ to his coronation.

9. The parenting programs _____ are very popular with young parents.

10. The five surveillance cameras _____ were installed last year.

54

Adjectival Phrases

Tick the sentence with an adjectival phrase.

1. (   ) The shoes in the yard are muddy.
   (   ) The muddy shoes are in the yard.

2. (   ) The man with the black umbrella was lurking outside our house.
   (   ) The man lurking outside our house had a black umbrella.

3. (   ) The ambulance sounding the siren is behind our bus.
   (   ) The ambulance behind our bus is sounding the siren.

4. (   ) The man in the hammock is having a nap.
   (   ) The man is having a nap in the hammock.

5. (   ) The park will be built beside our house soon.
   (   ) The empty land beside our house will be turned into a park soon.

Join each pair of sentences using an adjectival phrase.

6. The motorcycle is in the garage. It belongs to Uncle Vincent.

   _____

7. The beautiful actress looks familiar. She is on the stage.

   _____

8. The pot is made of earth. It is on the table.

   _____

9. These people work in the airline industry. They are on strike.

   _____

Linking Verbs

A **linking verb** shows a state of being rather than an action. It links, or connects, the subject of a sentence with a word or words in the predicate. The most common linking verbs are forms of **to be**, **to have** and **to seem**. Other examples of linking verbs, which could also act as ordinary verbs, are **appear**, **look**, **smell**, **taste**, **feel** and **grow**.

Underline the linking verb in each sentence.

1. After working on his report, he felt exhausted.

2. He decided to have some cake; it tasted great.

3. He refused to share the money and his brother seemed upset.

4. He was furious when he found out that his baby brother had knocked over the coffee and spoilt his computer.

5. He looked annoyed as he had to redo his report.

Put a ✓ in the brackets if the verb underlined is a linking verb.

6. (   ) The curry chicken <u>tasted</u> spicy.
   (   ) Mom <u>tasted</u> the spicy curry chicken.

7. (   ) The beanstalk <u>grew</u> so tall that it reached the clouds.
   (   ) He <u>grew</u> tired of waiting for his turn to play on the slide.

8. (   ) She <u>looked</u> at herself in the mirror after putting on her dress.
   (   ) She <u>looked</u> fine even though she had not slept for three nights.

9. (   ) The trumpeters <u>sounded</u> the trumpets loudly as the princess stepped onto the balcony.
   (   ) The music <u>sounded</u> so soothing that, before long, the children were fast asleep.

10. (   ) He <u>felt</u> disappointed that he could not go to Disneyland.
    (   ) He <u>felt</u> for his glasses in darkness.

Linking Verbs

Fill in the blanks with suitable linking verbs from the box. Use each word once only.

seemed	were	appeared
feel	is	looked

1. He _____ confused even though Mr Jacob had explained how to complete the exercise in detail.

2. They _____ hungry and tired after helping out at the restaurant the entire morning.

3. The children usually _____ sleepy after their swimming lesson.

4. He _____ excited to know that he has been selected to take part in the student-exchange program.

5. They _____ upset when they lost the match.

6. Our dog _____ sad despite all our effort to make it happy.

Underline the verb in each sentence. Write the verb on the line if it is a linking verb.

7. The bunny felt soft and cuddly. _____

8. The magician appeared in front of the audience. _____

9. She is gorgeous although she is already sixty. _____

10. The firefighters saved the lives of many people. _____

11. The fresh milk smells sour. _____

12. She feels nauseous after taking expired food. _____

Date: _____

Linking Verbs

Read each sentence. Fill in the bubble next to the linking verb.

1. Jayden thought the idea of having a barbecue was great.
   ○ thought   ○ was   ○ great

2. The barbecue chicken smelled delicious.
   ○ smelled   ○ delicious   ○ chicken

3. However, the sausages appeared burnt.
   ○ sausages   ○ burnt   ○ appeared

4. Mom seemed happy that everyone could attend the barbecue.
   ○ seemed   ○ happy   ○ attend

5. My relatives were excited to be there.
   ○ were   ○ be   ○ there

Underline the linking verb and circle the noun it describes.

6. Alice was surprised that her sister would take the plane again.

7. She always seemed frightened of going on flights.

8. Last time we took a flight, she felt nervous the moment the plane started moving.

9. She looked so pale that we thought she would faint.

10. We were worried about her and wanted to bring her to a doctor when the plane landed.

Verb Tenses

The **tense** of the verb shows the time of the action. The **present tense** shows that the action is happening now. The **past tense** shows that the action happened in the past. The **future tense** shows that the action will happen in the future.

Underline the verb forms in each sentence.

1. The dog barked loudly because a stranger approached the house.
2. We are planning to go to the park this evening.
3. She cries like a baby.
4. She has been waiting for the results of the test since last Monday.
5. Tommy had taken the candy from the table.
6. The policemen were patrolling the street when the old lady yelled for help.

Fill in the bubble next to the correct answer to complete each sentence.

7. Sally _____ the baby to the clinic as she was sick.
   - ○ brought
   - ○ had been bringing
   - ○ brings

8. The baby _____ when the needle went in.
   - ○ was crying
   - ○ has been crying
   - ○ cries

9. Sally _____ about the baby for the last few days as her fever never subsided.
   - ○ worried
   - ○ has been worrying
   - ○ had worried

10. The doctor said that the baby _____ well soon.
    - ○ gets
    - ○ got
    - ○ will get

11. Sally _____ better now that the baby is showing signs of recovery.
    - ○ felt
    - ○ feels
    - ○ will feel

Verb Tenses

Rewrite each sentence using the simple present, past or future tense of the verb as indicated below.

1. present: I walk to school every day.

   past: _____

   future: _____

2. present: _____

   past: _____

   future: Peter will eat cereal for breakfast tomorrow.

3. present: _____

   past: The children sang at the choir last Sunday.

   future: _____

4. present: _____

   past: Grandma baked a cake last Christmas.

   future: _____

5. present: The workers eat their lunch in the canteen every day.

   past: _____

   future: _____

Verb Tenses

Fill in the bubble next to the correct verb tense to complete the sentence.

1. Dylan _____ like a log. It is impossible to wake him up.
   ○ sleeps   ○ is sleeping   ○ has slept

2. Connie _____ for the competition tomorrow.
   ○ will dance   ○ has danced   ○ danced

3. Mike _____ with his toy car before Mom told him to do his homework.
   ○ was playing   ○ is playing   ○ played

4. Mom _____ for work after waving good-bye.
   ○ will be leaving ○ is leaving   ○ left

5. Miss Lee _____ to the student when she saw that he was hurt.
   ○ ran   ○ was running   ○ will run

Fill in the blanks with the correct tense of the verb in brackets.

6. Grandma _____ (keep) Grandpa's old albums for years before deciding to throw them away.

7. Daphne _____ (sing) like an angel at the Christmas concert last night.

8. We _____ (live) in Perth now, but we plan to relocate to Singapore soon.

9. Susan _____ (help) her mother at the shop for the last five years.

10. The pirates _____ (try) to hide before they were found out by the police.

Participles

A **participle** is a verb used as an adjective. The present participle form ends with **–ing**, and the past participle is formed differently depending on whether the verb is regular or irregular.

Write *present* if the underlined verb is a present participle or *past* if it is a past participle.

1. Having lost my wallet, I walked home instead
    of taking the taxi.   _____

2. I can't wait to read this underlined interesting book.   _____

3. Two hikers discovered an abandoned dog   _____

4. Having driven down this road many times,
    he did not need to ask for directions.   _____

5. The villagers offered him some cooked vegetables.   _____

Read each sentence and circle the participle(s).

6. After searching for five hours, the police finally found the bag of stolen money in the park.

7. Alex had a sprained ankle and was sent to the hospital.

8. The cat accidentally knocked over the pot of boiling water on the stove.

9. This sign tells you not to enter the forbidden area or else you will be in trouble.

10. It has been a long and tiring day, so I need to take a nap on the sofa.

11. Having set the table, Mom came out of the kitchen with smoked ham and a roasted turkey.

Participles

Change the verb in brackets to a participle and write it on the line.

1. The _____ (cry) child has been searching for his mother for the past half hour.

2. Vanessa seems _____ (worry) about her exams.

3. Having _____ (show) the admission ticket, Matthew quickly entered the concert hall.

4. He kept his parents _____ (wait) for him for a long time.

5. The objects must remain _____ (hide) and out of sight.

Circle the correct participle to complete the sentence.

6. The (drunk / drink / drinking) driver was caught by the police.

7. (Having tied / Tying / Tied) one end of the rope to the tree, Tom threw the other end into the river.

8. The (spoil / spoilt / has spoilt) child broke all the toys we gave him.

9. Snow (fell / fall / had fallen) everywhere and the roads had to be salted.

10. (Having slept / Sleep / Slept) for two whole hours, Alice woke up feeling energized.

Write two sentences using two different participles of the same verb.

11. _____

12. _____

Assessment

Participles

Fill in the bubble next to the correct answer to complete each sentence.

1. The instructions for building this robot _____ me, and I am not quite sure what to do.
   - ○ confuses
   - ○ confused
   - ○ have confused

2. There is a part of it missing as the pages have been _____.
   - ○ tear
   - ○ tore
   - ○ torn

3. Having _____ up trying to follow the manual, I decided to do it by trial and error.
   - ○ give
   - ○ gave
   - ○ given

4. I wondered if I should _____ my cousin to help me instead.
   - ○ get
   - ○ got
   - ○ have got

5. I finally decided to take the _____ robot to Jason, my cousin.
   - ○ break
   - ○ broke
   - ○ broken

6. _____ one look at the robot, he said he would help me.
   - ○ Take
   - ○ Took
   - ○ Taking

7. He kept me _____ while he wrote down a few notes on fixing robots that he thought might be useful for me.
   - ○ wait
   - ○ waiting
   - ○ waited

8. I went home and took out the notes that he had _____ and read through them.
   - ○ writes
   - ○ wrote
   - ○ written

Past Perfect Tense

The **past perfect tense** is used to talk about an action that was completed before another happened. It is formed with **_had_** + **_the past participle_**.

Read each sentence. Underline the verb in the past perfect tense.

1. I did not have any money as I had lost my wallet.

2. My parents had seen the house before they decided to buy it.

3. We were not able to get a hotel room as we had not booked one in advance.

4. Sam suddenly realized that he had left his English project at home.

5. The park looked awful as many people had dumped rubbish everywhere.

6. The couple had arranged a trip to Hawaii and could not attend the party.

Read each sentence. Decide if the underlined form of the verb needs to be changed into the past perfect tense. If it needs to be changed, write the correct answer on the line. If not, write an X.

7. Mr Brown <u>had served</u> in the army for ten years before he retired.

   _____

8. Grandma <u>forgot</u> to bring her key, so she could not get into the house.

   _____

9. After the students <u>clear</u> their lockers, they left school.   _____

10. After Dick <u>had saved</u> enough money, he bought a new car.   _____

11. The audience clapped loudly as the show was better
    than they <u>expected</u>.   _____

Past Perfect Tense

Read each sentence. Underline the first action and circle the second action.

1. Dad looked grumpy as Mom had discarded all his favorite car magazines.

2. After the students had done the experiment, they wrote a report on it.

3. Last Sunday, the customers had lined up outside this restaurant even before it opened for business.

4. The players waited until the referee blew the whistle.

5. A thief successfully broke into our house because we had not locked one of our windows properly.

Underline the correct word to complete each sentence.

6. (After / Before) my brother had finished typing the story, he switched off the computer.

7. Daisy quickly chose a beautiful white dress (after / before) she had walked into the boutique.

8. (After / Before) Dad took his car out for a drive, he had repaired it.

Join the two sentences together using the past tense and past perfect tense. Remember to use the correct punctuation.

9. Veronica dried the dishes. She put them away in the cupboard.

_____

10. The boy let go of the string. The balloon flew away.

_____

Past Perfect Tense

Fill in the bubble next to the correct answer to complete each sentence.

1. The party only started after the guest of honor _____ his entrance.
    ○ makes   ○ had made   ○ made

2. Even before he _____, the guests had eaten all the food.
    ○ arrived   ○ have arrived   ○ arrives

3. The organizers saw that food was running out and _____ to get more.
    ○ go   ○ went   ○ had gone

4. They made it back in time as they _____ the problem early on.
    ○ noticed   ○ had noticed   ○ notice

5. Before he _____ his speech, he thanked the organizers for giving him the opportunity to speak.
    ○ began   ○ had begun   ○ begins

6. The guest of honor, Mr Mako, _____ in Japan for many years before he migrated to Canada.
    ○ live   ○ had lived   ○ has lived

7. He _____ to Canada after he got a posting to work there.
    ○ migrates   ○ has migrated   ○ had migrated

8. He only _____ recognition for his inventions after many long years.
    ○ receives   ○ has received   ○ received

Past Perfect Continuous Tense

> The **past perfect continuous tense** is used when we talk about an
> action in the past that happened over a period of time. The form is
> **had been** + **verb** + **–ing**.

Read each sentence. Underline the past perfect continuous tense.

1. I did not understand the lesson because I had not been paying attention.

2. The company had been losing money for a few months, and now it has gone bankrupt.

3. The ground was wet as it had been raining.

4. Natalie had been having piano lessons since morning.

5. The poor boy fainted as he had not been eating for days.

6. Samantha's eyes were red as she had been weeping.

Read each sentence. Change the verb in brackets to the past perfect continuous tense and write it on the line.

7. Dad (paint) the door before the dog scratched it.   _____

8. The athletes needed a break, as they (exercise) the whole afternoon.   _____

9. The spectators (scream) at the top of their voices until the show came to an end.   _____

10. Many students failed the exam because they (not prepare) for it.   _____

11. My lower back ached, as I (ride) on the horse for two hours.   _____

12. Michelle looked really sunburnt, as she (lie) in the sun for too long.   _____

Past Perfect Continuous Tense

Read each sentence and underline the verb. Change the verb to the past perfect continuous tense and rewrite the sentence.

1. Rachel waited at the bus stop for two hours before it came.

   _____

2. The children looked forward to seeing her all week.

   _____

3. Michelle cared for them the past week, as Rachel was busy.

   _____

4. The children stood at the doorway for a long time.

   _____

5. They hoped to show her all the things they did during the week.

   _____

Answer each question using the past perfect continuous tense of the verb in brackets.

6. Why were you late for work?   (drive)

   _____

7. How did you find the dog?   (search)

   _____

8. Why did Vicky feel upset?   (argue)

   _____

Date: _____

Past Perfect Continuous Tense

Read each sentence. Fill in the bubble next to the correct answer to complete each sentence.

1. Melanie _____ English for two years before she went to England.
   - ○ has been learning
   - ○ had been learning
   - ○ learns

2. Professor Steele _____ at this university for more than twenty years before he retired.
   - ○ has been teaching
   - ○ had been teaching
   - ○ taught

3. Before Mom served dinner, she _____ in the kitchen for hours.
   - ○ was cooking
   - ○ had been cooking
   - ○ cooked

4. The little girl _____ all through the flight.
   - ○ was crying
   - ○ had been crying
   - ○ cries

5. Jason was exhausted as he _____.
   - ○ has been jogging
   - ○ had been jogging
   - ○ jogged

6. Joe _____ his car since eight this morning.
   - ○ has been cleaning
   - ○ had been cleaning
   - ○ cleaned

7. The boys _____ when the accident happened.
   - ○ were cycling
   - ○ had been cycling
   - ○ cycled

8. The baby _____ through the night and did not cry at all.
   - ○ is sleeping
   - ○ had been sleeping
   - ○ slept

9. They _____ for the magazine for the past five years.
   - ○ were writing
   - ○ had been writing
   - ○ have been writing

Future Tense

The **future tense** is used to talk about an action that will occur in the future. We use **will** or **be going to** to talk about the future or about an intention. We also use the present continuous tense to talk about what we have arranged to do in the future and **will be + verb + –ing** to talk about future action happening over a period of time.

Read each sentence. Underline the verb form that is used to express the future.

1. I am going to watch my favorite show on television tonight.

2. Carmen and Cathy will be busy for most of this summer.

3. My older brother is starting work in February.

4. Dad will be leaving for Taiwan next week.

5. I will be finishing university in June.

6. After college, Rachel is going to travel around the U.S.

Circle the correct verb form to express the future.

7. The window is open, and it is cold. I (will shut / will be shutting) the window.

8. Next Saturday, my cousin (is going to apply / is applying) for the job.

9. This time next Sunday, I (is lying / will be lying) on the beach and enjoying myself.

10. We (are having / will have) a party tomorrow; do join us!

11. Anne (will be staying / is staying) in France the whole of next summer.

Future Tense

Write a sentence for each situation, described in brackets, using the future tense.

1. (Express your intention to have a rest.)

    _____

2. (Talk about an event that will occur for a period of time in the future.)

    _____

3. (Talk about an arrangement to have a game of tennis with your friend the next day.)

    _____

4. (Express a decision to fix a leaking tap.)

    _____

Fill in the blanks with the future tense form of the verb in brackets.

5. Dad _____ (sell) the house once he finds a buyer for it.

6. I _____ (go) overseas to study for a year.

7. Tom _____ (work) tomorrow, so he will not be able to attend the party.

8. She _____ (meet) her mother at the front gate this afternoon.

9. We _____ (stay) at my cousin's house till our house is renovated.

10. I have decided that I _____ (attend) law school.

Future Tense

Fill in the bubble next to the correct answer to complete each sentence.

1. Minnie and Connie _____ on their Science project at school tomorrow.
    ○ will be working   ○ worked

2. I _____ the letter yesterday, before the post office closed for the day.
    ○ mailed   ○ am mailing

3. My friends _____ my birthday with me this Saturday.
    ○ are going to celebrate   ○ celebrate

4. I _____ my driving test tomorrow.
    ○ am taking   ○ have taken

5. The Moscow State Circus _____ in Cheltenham for the next two weeks.
    ○ will be performing   ○ are performing

6. The director of the company _____ the plan with his employees on Wednesday afternoon.
    ○ will discuss   ○ discuss

7. We _____ in a restaurant last week.
    ○ met   ○ will be meeting

8. I _____ some photos of this beautiful painting so that I can show them to her tomorrow.
    ○ will take   ○ took

More Verb Tenses

Read each sentence. Underline the verb form and write the tense of the verb on the line. Use *PS* for present simple, *PC* for present continuous, *PP* for present perfect and *PPC* for present perfect continuous.

1. I am getting the lunch ready.   _____

2. Rachel wakes up at six o'clock every morning.   _____

3. It is raining at the moment.   _____

4. The airplane has landed at the Pearson International Airport. _____

5. That burglar alarm has been ringing since eight o'clock
   this morning.   _____

6. I have cleaned the windows.   _____

Read each sentence. Underline the verb form and write the tense of the verb on the line. Use *PastS* for past simple, *PastC* for past continuous, *PastP* for past perfect and *PastPC* for past perfect continuous.

7. Natasha had been swimming in the pool.   _____

8. I had looked everywhere for my pencil case.   _____

9. Steve finally bought a new station wagon.   _____

10. My brother had been worrying about his exams all week.   _____

11. The light in the corridor was flashing.   _____

12. The wind had blown a tree over.   _____

More Verb Tenses

Read the conversation and decide if the underlined verb refers to the present or the future. Write it on the line below.

Mark: Hi Claire! What (1) <u>are</u> you <u>reading</u>?

Claire: Oh, it's a guidebook to France. I (2) <u>am going</u> there next month. My sister and I (3) <u>are having</u> a holiday there. I (4) <u>am</u> really <u>looking</u> forward to it. We (5) <u>are spending</u> three weeks in Paris. So, I (6) <u>am finding</u> out about all the things we can do there.

1. _____   4. _____

2. _____   5. _____

3. _____   6. _____

Fill in blanks with the correct form of the verb in brackets.

7. Kent and Kimberly could hear shouts from the flat next door. Their neighbors _____ (argue) again.

8. The television in the living room was still on although there was no one there. Someone _____ (watch) it.

9. When I saw Uncle Ben last week, he said he _____ (stop) smoking. But when I saw him two days later, he _____ (smoke) a cigarette.

10. When Mandy _____ (arrive) at my house, I was lying on the sofa reading a detective novel.

11. Sarah _____ (buy) a new mobile phone last Saturday. She finds it very useful. She _____ (use) it all the time.

More Verb Tenses

Fill in the bubble next to the correct tense of the underlined verb.

1. He broke his leg when he <u>was skiing</u>.
   - ○ past simple
   - ○ past continuous
   - ○ present simple
   - ○ present continuous

2. Mark <u>has changed</u> his mind about dining out tonight.
   - ○ past perfect
   - ○ past continuous
   - ○ present perfect
   - ○ present continuous

3. I <u>have been ironing</u> the clothes since ten o'clock this morning.
   - ○ past perfect
   - ○ past continuous
   - ○ present perfect
   - ○ present perfect continuous

4. The runners needed a rest as they <u>had been running</u> all day.
   - ○ past perfect
   - ○ present perfect
   - ○ past perfect continuous
   - ○ present perfect continuous

Fill in the bubble next to the correct verb form to complete each sentence.

5. I'm busy at the moment, as I _____ on the computer.
   - ○ work
   - ○ am working
   - ○ worked

6. Bill _____ sick for two weeks. He's still in the hospital.
   - ○ had been
   - ○ has been
   - ○ was

7. Matthew _____ tennis every Saturday afternoon.
   - ○ will be playing
   - ○ is playing
   - ○ plays

8. Vicky _____ a beautiful dream when the alarm clock rang.
   - ○ was having
   - ○ has been having
   - ○ had

9. They _____ all their work last week.
   - ○ had completed
   - ○ were completing
   - ○ complete

Adverbs

An **adverb** is a word that adds information about the action, event or situation mentioned in a clause. It can be added to a verb to modify its meaning or to make it clearer or more exact.

Underline the adverb in each sentence.

1. My brother slammed the door angrily and locked himself in his bedroom.

2. Henry is 18 years old, and he is almost as tall as his dad.

3. Mom parked her car slowly in the garage.

4. Grandma probably left her purple handbag on the bus.

5. I don't think my colleague is around as he is usually late for work.

6. The cook mixed all the ingredients well before cooking.

Read each sentence. Underline the verb or adjective that the adverb modifies.

7. The lion walked stealthily towards the deer.

8. Bianca wore a beautifully decorated dress to the party.

9. The heavenly blue light was shining on the water.

10. Angel is an exceptionally talented dancer and needs to practice several hours every day.

11. I am sweating because today's weather is extremely hot.

12. The very old man wakes up at four o'clock every morning and walks slowly to the park.

Adverbs

Read each sentence and write the adverb on the line.

1. Tina danced in gracefully from the wings
   to the center stage.   _____

2. My sister was terribly sorry for wearing my favorite
   dress without asking me.   _____

3. I had been waiting at the clinic for three hours
   and finally got the chance to see the doctor.   _____

4. The bride was surprised that all the guests arrived
   early for her wedding ceremony.   _____

5. Sandra walked past us, but she didn't say hello.   _____

Read each sentence. Change the word in brackets to an adverb and
write it on the line.

6. My brother broke the vase and apologised (immediate). _____

7. Tom fell down the stairs and his ankle was (bad) bruised.   _____

8. Today, the U.S. government announced that they had
   (successful) launched a rocket carrying a satellite. _____

9. In the library, the man was asked by the librarian not
   to talk (loud) with his friend.   _____

10. My yoga teacher told me to (slight) bend down and
    grab hold of my ankles.   _____

11. Mom held my hand (firm) and led me across the road. _____

Adverbs

Fill in the bubble next to the adverb used in each sentence.

1. Marcus will eventually find a job that he enjoys doing.
   ○ eventually   ○ find   ○ enjoys

2. The suspect wearily explained to the police that he had not been in the house when the murder happened.
   ○ suspect   ○ wearily   ○ murder

3. Have you played chess recently?
   ○ played   ○ recently   ○ chess

4. My parents have definitely decided on where to go for our vacation.
   ○ definitely   ○ decided   ○ vacation

Fill in the bubble next to the correct adverb to complete each sentence.

5. Miss Wong _____ doesn't allow her students to bring mobile phones to school.
   ○ certainly   ○ certain

6. When we arrived, I _____ remembered that I had forgotten my admission ticket.
   ○ suddenly   ○ sudden

7. Mandy _____ tripped over a rock and hurt her knee.
   ○ accident   ○ accidentally

8. I was _____ surprised when I opened the door to see Mark with a bunch of roses in his hand.
   ○ delightful   ○ delightfully

9. He wolfed down the sandwich _____.
   ○ hungry   ○ hungrily

Intensifiers

An **intensifier** is a word that is placed before or after an adjective or adverb to make its meaning stronger or weaker.

Read each sentence. Circle the intensifier.

1. The weather in the Arctic is extremely cold.

2. Gina is absolutely right in bringing a mobile phone when hiking.

3. Throwing rubbish out of the window is totally unacceptable.

4. Jamie had a sore throat and her voice was barely audible.

5. Grandma was really ill and had to stay in the hospital for a week.

6. Mark looked rather upset after being scolded by his teacher.

Fill in the blanks using *a bit, quite* or *very.*

7. There were small traces of mud on the boots. They were _____ dirty.

8. The bus was almost on time. It was just _____ late.

9. Steve paid a huge sum of money for his house. It was _____ expensive.

10. There was a medium amount of traffic on the road. It was _____ busy.

11. Karen couldn't sleep because of the awful noise. The people on the streets were _____ noisy.

12. The weather was all right – at least it didn't rain. It was _____ good.

Intensifiers

Read each sentence. Circle the intensifier and underline the adjective or adverb it qualifies.

1. I was extremely angry when I saw a man treating his dog cruelly on the street.

2. Time passed quite quickly and we all had fun at the park.

3. This bed is uncomfortable because it is too hard.

4. As an educator, I understand that each person learns in a slightly different way.

5. The company will not hire Annie as she is not experienced enough for the job.

Read each sentence. The intensifier is given in brackets. Rewrite the sentence on the line putting the intensifier in the correct place.

6. That radio is loud. (a bit)

    _____

7. The team did the job quickly. (fairly)

    _____

8. This dress is not big. (enough)

    _____

9. I feel better now. (a lot)

    _____

10. This drawing is perfect. (almost)

    _____

Intensifiers

Read each sentence and identify the intensifier. Fill in the bubble next to the correct answer.

1. Just give me another minute. I'm almost ready to leave for our trip.
    ○ almost   ○ ready   ○ leave

2. These clothes, which have been kept in the attic for a long time, are very old.
    ○ long   ○ very   ○ old

3. We need to drive Uncle Ben home as he is completely exhausted.
    ○ completely   ○ drive   ○ exhausted

4. My brother is so annoying when he screams.
    ○ annoying   ○ screams   ○ so

Fill in the bubble next to the most suitable intensifier to complete each sentence.

5. The company offers a great variety of _____ luxurious cars equipped with leather seats and the latest technology.
    ○ a bit   ○ rather   ○ really

6. Harvard University is an established university with a _____ good reputation and a long history.
    ○ fairly   ○ quite   ○ very

7. I am _____ lost, and I don't think I will be get out of this place.
    ○ totally   ○ rather   ○ slightly

8. The bus service is reliable, and the buses are _____ frequent.
    ○ quite   ○ very   ○ a bit

Connectors

Connectors are joining words used to combine two or more words, phrases or sentences.

Read each sentence. Circle the connector.

1. Emma wanted to go into the tomb despite knowing how dangerous it is.

2. I accidentally dropped the dish, but it didn't break.

3. You can choose to walk up the stairs or take the escalator to the second floor.

4. Many customers like to shop in this boutique although the clothes are expensive.

5. The music was loud, nevertheless it was enjoyable.

6. Susan left halfway through the movie because she didn't enjoy it.

Underline the most suitable connector to complete each sentence.

7. Max decided to buy the bicycle (although / but / and) it was expensive.

8. Cooking is my favorite hobby, (and / but / because) I am too busy to cook.

9. Clare was ill, (or / but / and) she insisted on being present at the meeting.

10. You won't lose weight (since / unless / therefore) you control your diet.

11. We could go swimming (or / and / but) jogging.

12. This house is located in a quiet area (nevertheless / despite / whereas) that house is on a busy street.

Connectors

Use the connector in brackets to combine the sentences. Write the new sentence on the line.

1. Ernest wants to eat at home. His wife wants to dine out.   (but)

   _____

2. Our receptionist answers phone calls. She greets customers.   (and)

   _____

3. Annie said nothing. She was too angry to speak.   (because)

   _____

Use a suitable connector that is related to time from the box to replace the one in brackets. Write it on the line to complete each sentence.

before	while	when
until	since	as soon as

4. Mark heard the news on the radio _____ (during the time) he was driving home.

5. I went straight to my friend's house _____ (immediately after) I left the airport.

6. You need to stir with a spoon _____ (up to the time) the sugar dissolves.

7. I must get to the classroom _____ (earlier than) the bell rings.

8. My leg really hurts _____ (at the time) I walk.

9. Ellie hasn't been able to work _____ (from the time) the day she fell ill.

Date: _____

Connectors

Read each sentence. Fill in the bubble next to the connector.

1. Bob is very tall whereas his twin brother Bill is very short.
   - ○ very
   - ○ is
   - ○ whereas

2. Dad refused to sign the contract until all the amendments were done.
   - ○ until
   - ○ amendments
   - ○ done

3. Please answer the door while I'm cooking in the kitchen.
   - ○ answer
   - ○ while
   - ○ cooking

4. The weather forecast said it would rain, but it turned out to be a beautiful day.
   - ○ would
   - ○ be
   - ○ but

Fill in the bubble next to the most suitable connector to complete each sentence.

5. You can't drive a car _____ you've got a license.
   - ○ unless
   - ○ despite
   - ○ but

6. Mr Wong didn't hire Emma _____ she was qualified for the job.
   - ○ as long as
   - ○ although
   - ○ because

7. Lincoln was late for work again _____ the warning given by his manager.
   - ○ in case
   - ○ despite
   - ○ and

8. We decided to order food delivery _____ we were too tired to cook.
   - ○ so
   - ○ but
   - ○ because

Compound Sentences

> A **compound sentence** is a sentence made up of two simple sentences and the conjunction **and**, **but** or **or**.

Circle the conjunction in brackets that best completes each sentence. Then, rewrite the sentence using the conjunction.

1. I want to go to the movies, _____ my friend Pat does not. (or / but)

   _____

2. It rained last night, _____ we had to stay home. (and / but)

   _____

3. Ed will drive to Texas, _____ he will take the train. (or / and)

   _____

4. It snowed this morning, _____ the sun came out in the afternoon. (but / or)

   _____

Write a compound sentence with the two simple sentences using the conjunction in brackets.

5. We wanted to ride our bikes home. Mine had a flat tire. (but)

   _____

6. The whistle blew. The train pulled out of the station. (and)

   _____

7. I will finish the job today. Bob will finish it tomorrow. (or)

   _____

Compound Sentences

In the space provided, combine each pair of sentences to form one compound sentence. Use a comma, if necessary, and choose the conjunction (*and, but* or *or*) that makes most sense.

1. Our cousins arrived. We were very happy to see them.

    _____

2. Eileen had cut her hair short. Her twin sister Emily still had long hair.

    _____

3. They had always looked exactly alike. I could not get used to them.

    _____

4. Would they play with me? Would they play only with my older sisters?

    _____

5. First, Eileen gave me a hug. Then, Emily did the same.

    _____

6. Our parents went into the kitchen to talk. The rest of us preferred to be outside.

    _____

7. At dinner, Mom said the twins could stay with us. We could go stay with them.

    _____

Compound Sentences

Decide if there is an error in the underlined part of each compound sentence.
Fill in the bubble next to the correct answer.

1. We cleaned our house last <u>weekend, and I</u> threw out some old books and toys.
    ○ weekend but I   ○ weekend or I   ○ correct as is

2. Old toys went in a big plastic <u>bag, but old books</u> went in a box.
    ○ bag or old books   ○ bag, old books   ○ correct as is

3. I could have cleared my <u>bookshelf, and I</u> wanted to keep a few old favorites.
    ○ bookshelf, but I   ○ bookshelf, or I   ○ correct as is

4. I gave some toys to a <u>neighbor, but most</u> went to the thrift store.
    ○ neighbor or most   ○ neighbor and most   ○ correct as is

5. We drove to the thrift <u>store, and I</u> helped carry the boxes inside.
    ○ store or I   ○ store but I   ○ correct as is

Fill in the blanks with *and, but* or *or.*

6. I wanted to look around the store, _____ we didn't have time.

7. I saw an old typewriter there, _____ no one uses those
    things anymore!

8. We could have stopped at the library _____ had a snack at the coffee shop.

9. My shelves looked empty, _____ the library books helped fill them
    up a little.

10. I loved my old books, _____ my interests have changed as I've
    gotten older.

Complex Sentences

A **complex sentence** is a sentence with one independent clause and at least one dependent clause. It has a subordinator, such as **because**, **since**, **after** and **although**, and relative pronouns, such as **that**, **who** and **which**.

Read the following sentences. Underline the complex sentences.

1. The movie was well-filmed although it was quite long.

2. It was about the survival of a boy at sea.

3. Since the movie was directed by a famous director, we decided that we had to watch it.

4. The boy who played the main character also received an award for his superb performance.

5. After he won the award, he received a lot of offers to star in other movies.

6. We thoroughly enjoyed the movie and hope to watch more movies by the same director.

Read each sentence. Underline the independent clause.

7. The teacher returned the homework after she had noticed the mistake.

8. The students are busy studying because they have a test tomorrow.

9. John and Maria went out to watch a movie after they had finished revising.

10. You have to wait until the light changes to green.

11. I must get to the post office before it closes.

Complex Sentences

Read each sentence. Circle the subordinator.

1. Karen's eyesight was normal until she was 15 months of age.

2. I'll go visit Grandpa in the hospital when I finish my work.

3. We'd better allow plenty of time for the journey because there may be a traffic jam.

4. Victor will take the CD player back to the shop if it doesn't work.

Read each sentence. Underline the independent clause once and the dependent clause twice.

5. Aesop wrote a story about a shepherd boy who was protecting a flock of sheep from a wolf.

6. The students left the playground early because it started to rain.

7. The cat licked her paws after she had played with the yarn.

8. Fighting infection was difficult until penicillin was discovered.

9. Grandma gave her house key to me to keep because she trusted me.

10. The Great Barrier Reef is the world's largest reef which contains an abundance of marine life.

Write a complex sentence. Underline the independent clause and circle the dependent clause.

11. _____

_____

Complex Sentences

Fill in the bubble that tells if the underlined part of the sentence is an independent or dependent clause.

1. My baby brother is very grumpy <u>when he does not get enough sleep</u>.
   - ○ independent clause   ○ dependent clause

2. <u>Prudence visits the humane society</u> because she loves animals.
   - ○ independent clause   ○ dependent clause

3. <u>Sam went to work</u> although he did not feel well.
   - ○ independent clause   ○ dependent clause

4. <u>We had to cancel our visit to the zoo</u> because of the heavy rain.
   - ○ independent clause   ○ dependent clause

5. My dog caught the Frisbee <u>when I threw it in the air</u>.
   - ○ independent clause   ○ dependent clause

Read each sentence. Fill in the bubble next to the subordinator.

6. I'm sure I know the person who is standing over there.
   - ○ person   ○ who   ○ standing

7. My phone is out of order, which is a real nuisance.
   - ○ phone   ○ nuisance   ○ which

8. Lily couldn't find the box that she kept her photos in.
   - ○ kept   ○ photos   ○ that

9. This is the place where the accident happened.
   - ○ place   ○ where   ○ accident

10. I like to travel at night when the roads are quiet.
    - ○ roads   ○ at   ○ when

Using *If*

A **conditional sentence** talks about an action that can only take place if a certain condition is fulfilled. There are three different types of conditional sentences. See the table below.

Conditional Type	Conditional Form
first conditional: when the condition is likely to be fulfilled	*if* + simple present, *will* + verb
second conditional: when the condition is unlikely to be fulfilled	*if* + simple past, *would / could / might* + verb
third conditional: when the condition is impossible to be fulfilled because it refers to the past	*if* + past perfect, *would / could / might have* + past participle

Read each sentence and decide if it is a first, second or third conditional. Write the answer on the line.

1. If you had arrived on time, we would have caught the train. _____

2. If I were you, I would seek advice from a lawyer. _____

3. If Ronny had my phone number, he could have contacted me. _____

4. If Sam had found a calculator, he could have worked out the sums a lot quicker. _____

5. If it rains, the school will cancel our picnic. _____

6. If you study hard, you will get a good result in your English exam. _____

7. If Daniel has money, he will buy the book at the bookshop. _____

8. If Rita had taken better care of her plants, they would not have died. _____

Using *If*

Draw a line to match the clauses.

1.	If you win the game,	•	•	we would have had a ride on the roller coaster.
2.	If I went to bed earlier,	•	•	I would have difficulty falling asleep.
3.	If you had come to the theme park with us,	•	•	you could take a photo.
4.	If you brought your camera,	•	•	you might have enjoyed it.
5.	If you had watched the movie,	•	•	I will buy you lunch.

Read each sentence. Fill in the blank with the correct form of the verb given in brackets.

6. If I find Connie's address, I _____ (send) her an invitation to my party.

7. If you _____ (swallow) the washing detergent, it would have killed you.

8. If my brother had a dictionary, he _____ (check) the meaning of the word.

9. If Kim had come to school today, I _____ (lend) her my book.

10. If I _____ (forget) my best friend's birthday, she will feel upset and disappointed.

11. If my back _____ (ache) tomorrow, I will stay at home.

Assessment

Using *If*

Identify the type of conditional sentence. Fill in the bubble next to the correct answer.

1. If John had played in the match, his team might have won the gold medal.
   ○ first   ○ second   ○ third

2. If Fanny feels unwell, she will stay home.
   ○ first   ○ second   ○ third

3. If you had made a reservation, we would have gotten a table.
   ○ first   ○ second   ○ third

4. If people used public transport, there would be less pollution.
   ○ first   ○ second   ○ third

5. If you put too many books in the paper bag, it will burst.
   ○ first   ○ second   ○ third

Fill in the bubble next to the correct answer to complete each sentence.

6. If Melissa had phoned me, I _____ her some help.
   ○ could give   ○ could have given   ○ will give

7. If my brother _____ Mom's favorite china bowl, Mom will be very cross.
   ○ break   ○ breaks   ○ broke

8. If Uncle Ben _____ to Hong Kong, I would ask him to stay at our house.
   ○ come   ○ came   ○ had come

9. If Jeremy _____ to Janice, she will marry him.
   ○ would propose   ○ proposed   ○ proposes

Word Order

A simple sentence or statement begins with the subject and then introduces the verb. This is called **word order**. There are three main structures which we can use to make a simple sentence:

1. subject + verb
   (e.g. *I*) (e.g. *move*)
2. subject + verb + object
   (e.g. *I*) (e.g. *move*) (e.g. *the chair*)
3. subject + verb + complement (adjective or noun phrase)
   (e.g. *It*) (e.g. *is*) (e.g. *big / a big problem*)

Read each sentence. Underline the subject, circle the verb and put brackets around the object or complement.

1. Elvin is chewing gum.

2. The tower is tall.

3. I am eating.

4. My leg has a big wound.

5. My teacher told a story.

6. The turtle is laying eggs.

Read each sentence. Look at the underlined words and identify what part of the sentence it is – subject, verb, object or complement. Write it on the line.

7. Ivana bought <u>a necklace</u>. _____

8. I <u>am swimming</u>. _____

9. <u>My boots</u> are muddy. _____

10. Our trip was <u>a wonderful experience</u>. _____

11. Richard <u>enjoys</u> camping. _____

Word Order

The following is a conversation between five people after they have moved a piano. Read each piece of dialogue and indentify the type of sentence structure. Write the letter(s) on the lines below.

a) Ben: That was a difficult job.

b) Tom: I agree.

c) Sam: The piano is heavy.

d) Tim: We need a rest.

e) Ian: My arms are aching.

1. subject + verb _____

2. subject + verb + object _____

3. subject + verb + complement _____

Put the words in the correct order and write the statement on the line. Remember to use the correct punctuation.

4. looks / Molly / pale

_____

5. a great time / we / are having

_____

6. an accident / Daniel / had

_____

7. ice cream / are eating / the children

_____

Word Order

Fill in the bubble that tells which part of the sentence the underlined words are.

1. Johnny won a <u>medal</u>.
   ○ subject   ○ verb   ○ object   ○ complement

2. My brother is <u>chubby</u>.
   ○ subject   ○ verb   ○ object   ○ complement

3. It was <u>a good idea</u>.
   ○ subject   ○ verb   ○ object   ○ complement

4. I <u>am watching</u> a movie.
   ○ subject   ○ verb   ○ object   ○ complement

What is the structure of each of the following sentences? Fill in the bubble next to the correct answer.

5. Mom is feeding the baby.
   ○ subject + verb   ○ subject + verb + object
   ○ subject + verb + complement

6. The gorilla is strong.
   ○ subject + verb   ○ subject + verb + object
   ○ subject + verb + complement

7. I sneezed.
   ○ subject + verb   ○ subject + verb + object
   ○ subject + verb + complement

8. New York City is a busy city.
   ○ subject + verb   ○ subject + verb + object
   ○ subject + verb + complement

More about Word Order

> There are two other structures that we can use to make a statement.
>
> 1. subject + verb + adverbial (a prepositional phrase or an adverb)
>   (e.g. **It**)   (e.g. **is**)   (e.g. **on my foot / nearby**)
>
> 2. subject + verb + indirect object + direct object
>   (e.g. **I**)   (e.g. **bought**)   (e.g. **Mom**)   (e.g. **a present**)

Read each sentence. Underline the adverbial.

1. The cat is sitting on the porch.

2. My brother laughed loudly.

3. Susan left with a smile.

4. Bob works at the grocery store.

5. I fell accidentally.

6. Clement was travelling in a taxi.

Read each sentence. Look at the underlined words and tell what part of the sentence it is – subject, verb, adverbial or object. Write it on the line.

7. The spider <u>is crawling</u> on the wall. _____

8. It's giving me <u>a headache</u>. _____

9. I sent <u>my friend</u> a postcard. _____

10. The Chan family live <u>on a farm</u>. _____

11. <u>Mrs Wilson</u> gave the class a quiz. _____

12. The puppy is sleeping <u>in the kennel</u>. _____

More about Word Order

Look at each sentence and identify the type of sentence structure. Write the letters on the line.

a)   Mom is telling me a story.

b)   The baby slept through the night.

c)   Aunt Stella baked me a cake.

d)   The students sat on the lawn.

e)   Natalie lent Steven her Math textbook.

f)   I gave my friend some help.

1.   subject + verb + adverbial _____

2.   subject + verb + indirect object + direct object _____

Rewrite each sentence correctly on the line.

3.   Mom buy a teddy will bear.

   _____

4.   Nearby is Connie's house.

   _____

5.   The eagle in the sky is flying.

   _____

Write a sentence of your own. Underline the subject, circle the verb and put brackets around the adverbial or indirect and direct objects.

6.   _____

More about Word Order

Fill in the bubble that tells which part of the sentence the underlined words are.

1. Emma told me <u>a joke</u>.
   - ○ subject
   - ○ direct object
   - ○ verb
   - ○ indirect object

2. My students <u>were waiting</u> at the bus stop.
   - ○ subject
   - ○ direct object
   - ○ verb
   - ○ adverbial

3. The car stopped <u>at the lights</u>.
   - ○ subject
   - ○ direct object
   - ○ verb
   - ○ adverbial

4. <u>Lisa</u> made me a brooch.
   - ○ subject
   - ○ direct object
   - ○ verb
   - ○ indirect object

Rewrite each sentence correctly on the line.

5. The couple their wedding anniversary was celebrating at the restaurant.

   _____

6. We gave a special cake the couple.

   _____

7. The man a bouquet of flowers gave the lady.

   _____

8. She bought a tie him.

   _____

Active and Passive Voice

> A sentence is said to be in the **active voice** if the subject performs the action expressed by the verb. A sentence is said to be in the **passive voice** if the action is performed on the subject. We often use the passive voice when the subject is not important.
>
> Example: They have found a cure for cancer. (active voice)
>   A cure for cancer has been found. (passive voice)

Read each sentence. Write *active* if the sentence is in the active voice and *passive* if it is in the passive voice.

1.   People have seen foxes on the streets of London.   _____

2.   Tiffany sent a photograph of a fox to her grandparents.   _____

3.   The reason for the phenomenon has not been found.   _____

4.   The foxes are causing problems in the city.   _____

5.   The issue is being discussed by scientists.   _____

6.   Many suspect that humans are to blame.   _____

Read each sentence. Underline the subject.

7.   Mom baked the bread yesterday.

8.   The puppy will be fed by Christine at noon.

9.   On our way home, we were stopped by the police.

10. The famous painting, *Mona Lisa,* was painted by Leonardo da Vinci in the sixteenth century.

11. The thief snatched my phone and ran away.

12. The debate was organized by the sponsors.

Active and Passive Voice

Change the sentences from active voice to passive voice.

1. We decorated the house for Christmas.

   _____

2. Cheryl sent out the invites for the party.

   _____

3. My parents cooked the delicious spread.

   _____

4. My cousins brought the beautiful flowers.

   _____

Change the sentences from passive voice to active voice.

5. The event was organized by various charitable organizations.

   _____

6. The topics were discussed by a panel of experts.

   _____

7. Different solutions were presented by each group.

   _____

8. Outside the venue, protests were held by various groups.

   _____

Active and Passive Voice

Fill in the bubble next to the person or thing that performs the action.

1. James interviewed more than a hundred applicants for the job.
   ○ James   ○ applicants   ○ interviewed

2. The applicants were later interviewed by the manager.
   ○ manager   ○ interviewed   ○ applicants

3. The applicants completed a few forms.
   ○ forms   ○ applicants   ○ completed

4. These certificates were submitted by the applicants.
   ○ submitted   ○ certificates   ○ applicants

Change the sentences from active voice to passive voice and vice versa.

5. The villagers were rescued from the fire by the firefighters.

   _____

6. The police suspect a teenager of committing arson.

   _____

7. After four months, they caught the suspect.

   _____

8. The incident was reported in the news by a reporter.

   _____

9. The villagers rebuilt their homes after many months.

   _____

Direct and Indirect Speech

In **direct speech**, we quote the exact words that the speaker uses and put quotation marks around these words. We use **indirect speech** to report what a person has said. If the speech contains a **present tense verb**, we often change it to the **past tense**. We often need to change the **pronouns** too.

Decide if each sentence is in direct or indirect speech. Write *direct* if it is in direct speech and *indirect* if it is in indirect speech.

1. Sam asked, "Have you seen any good movies recently?" _____

2. "I left my camera in the taxi!" Gareth exclaimed. _____

3. Tom said that he would pay the bill. _____

4. Carrie said that she was munching on an apple. _____

Complete each pair of sentences with the correct form of speech.

5. Daniel said, "I went for a job interview yesterday."

   Daniel said that he had gone for a job interview _____.

6. Christine asked, "How did the interview go?"

   Christine asked how the interview _____.

7. "Was the interviewer friendly?" asked Joel.

   Joel _____ if the interviewer had been friendly.

8. "Yes, she was friendly," said Daniel.

   Daniel said that _____.

Direct and Indirect Speech

Change the following sentences from direct speech to indirect speech and vice versa.

1. "I'm busy fixing the bookshelf," said Alex.

   _____

2. Leo said he had been studying Spanish for one year.

   _____

3. "Mom has cleaned the windows already," said my sister.

   _____

4. "I'm meeting my friend at the station tomorrow," said Dan.

   _____

Complete each pair of sentences with the correct form of speech.

5. "I had my eye test last week," said Rachel.
   Rachel said that she had had her eye test _____.

6. "The conference was last week," said my sister.
   My sister told me that the conference had taken place _____.

7. "I hope that I can pass my test," said Gina.
   Gina said that _____ hoped that _____.

8. "Could you please leave some food for me?" asked Joseph.
   Joseph asked me to leave some food for _____.

Direct and Indirect Speech

Change each sentence from direct to indirect speech and vice versa. Fill in the bubble next to the correct answer.

1. "I'm having tea with May," said Jane.
   - ○ Jane said that I was having tea with May.
   - ○ Jane said that she was having tea with May.
   - ○ Jane said that she is having tea with May.

2. "Tom has sent a postcard to me," said Joe.
   - ○ Joe said that Tom had sent a postcard to him.
   - ○ Joe said that Tom has sent a postcard to him.
   - ○ Joe said that Tom had sent a postcard to me.

3. Kim said she had passed her Math examination.
   - ○ "I have passed her Math examination," said Kim.
   - ○ "I had passed her Math examination," said Kim.
   - ○ "I have passed my Math examination," said Kim.

4. The couple said they wanted to get married.
   - ○ "We want to get married," said the couple.
   - ○ "They wanted to get married," said the couple.
   - ○ "We wanted to get married," said the couple.

Rewrite each sentence as indirect speech.

5. Paul said, "I have forgotten to close the windows."

   _____

6. Janice asked, "Can you help me buy movie tickets?"

   _____

7. Justin said, "I'll do it tomorrow."

   _____

Prepositions

> **Prepositions** tell us how a noun or pronoun relates to another. Groups of words introduced by a preposition are called **prepositional phrases**.

Underline the prepositional phrase in each sentenece.

1. Take the set of keys that are on the counter.

2. Bring me the boxes below the table.

3. Above the cabinet hangs the wall clock.

4. I left you a slice of cake in the silver pan.

5. Shine the light into the room.

Fill in the blank with a suitable preposition.

6. Melanie will invite her friends _____ her house in April.

7. She will send out the invites _____ the housewarming party.

8. She went _____ the store to find some nice decorations.

9. She walked _____ the different aisles but could not find anything she really liked.

10. She finally found some beautiful streamers _____ the top shelves.

11. She hung them _____ the entrance doors.

12. She tied bunches of balloons _____ the corners of the room.

Prepositions

Read each sentence. Underline the preposition(s).

1. Janice dropped the coin, and it rolled under the sofa.

2. I drove past the mountains and through the tunnel.

3. The temperature outside is now above thirty degree Celsius.

4. Sam accidentally pushed me into the swimming pool, and I almost drowned.

5. There was a huge crowd in the stadium waiting for the Olympic Games to start.

6. I could hear someone running behind me, and I turned around to see that it was my friend.

Read the following conversation and decide if you should put a preposition in the blank. If yes, put in the correct preposition; if not, put an *X*.

7. Daniel: I'm sorry that I was out when you called _____ yesterday afternoon. I'm free _____ the thirteenth of February. Can we meet then?

8. Daisy: But I'm busy _____ next week. I don't think I can meet you _____ Friday.

9. Daniel: I would like to have a meeting with you _____ this month if possible.

10. Daisy: I will be out of town _____ Easter, so how about the week after?

11. Daniel: I've got an appointment _____ the morning on the twenty-eighth. Can we meet _____ the afternoon _____ half-past three?

Date: _____

Prepositions

Fill in the bubble next to the correct preposition to complete each sentence.

1. Dad was wearing a long black coat that came down well _____ his knees.
    - ○ below
    - ○ under
    - ○ after

2. I think I'll get a necklace _____ Mom on Mother's Day.
    - ○ to
    - ○ by
    - ○ for

3. We finally got _____ the bus and ran quickly to the entrance of the park.
    - ○ off
    - ○ of
    - ○ over

4. Libya is located _____ Algeria and Egypt in Africa.
    - ○ beside
    - ○ below
    - ○ between

Choose a suitable preposition from the box to fill in the blank. Each one can only be used once.

to	off	on	across	down	under

5. I found a spot _____ a tree and lay _____ the grass to rest.

6. While Dad was climbing _____ the ladder, he fell _____ and hurt his legs.

7. Chester, who was standing on the other side of the road, beckoned _____ me, so I walked _____ the road and had a chat with him.

Date: _____

Phrasal Verbs

A **phrasal verb** is a verb plus a preposition or adverb, which conveys a meaning different from that of the original verb.

Read each sentence and find the phrasal verb(s). Circle the verb and underline the preposition or adverb.

1. The plane took off late because of the stormy weather.

2. You should carry on writing your essay.

3. The rocket blasted off at 5 p.m. this afternoon.

4. Well done! Keep up the excellent effort!

5. The government has closed down most of the coal mines.

6. Mr Smith has carved out a successful career in the building industry.

Choose a suitable preposition or adverb from the box to complete the phrasal verb in the sentence. The meaning is given in brackets for your help.

to	off	on	down	out

7. Sarah put _____ a few pounds. (Sarah gained some weight.)

8. Keep it _____ yourself. (Don't tell anyone about it.)

9. I'm sorry that I let you _____. (I'm sorry that I disappointed you.)

10. Many students dropped _____ because they did not enjoy the course. (Many students withdrew from the course.)

11. Dad dozed _____ on the sofa. (Dad fell into a light sleep on the sofa.)

Phrasal Verbs

Read each sentence. Choose the phrasal verb from the box that can replace the underlined word and write it on the line. Change the tense of the verb if necessary.

looking into	fall out	send out
set up	put off	cut in

1. Mr Smith <u>postponed</u> the meeting until next week. _____

2. The police are still <u>investigating</u> the cause of the explosion which badly damaged a building in the city yesterday. _____

3. It is urgent that we <u>distribute</u> the revised circular to the parents to notify them about the changes. _____

4. Please do not <u>quarrel</u> over such a small matter! _____

5. I do not wish to <u>interrupt</u>, but this is really important. _____

6. The director of the company decided to <u>establish</u> a new sales office in New York. _____

What does the underlined phrasal verb in each sentence mean? Draw a line to match the phrasal verb to the correct meaning.

7.	Carmen hurt her knee and <u>broke down</u> in tears.	•	•	failed
8.	My car <u>broke down</u>, so I took a taxi to work.	•	•	started crying
9.	The firemen <u>broke down</u> the door of the house.	•	•	stopped working
10.	Amanda's marriage <u>broke down</u> after three years.	•	•	hit hard and opened

Date: _____

Phrasal Verbs

Fill in the bubble next to the phrasal verb that explains the underlined word.

1. Bonnie's grandmother suddenly died, so she had to <u>cancel</u> her wedding.
   - ○ call away
   - ○ call off
   - ○ call down

2. My old school will be <u>demolished</u> as it is too dilapidated.
   - ○ pull through
   - ○ pull off
   - ○ pull down

3. Someone must have <u>triggered</u> the smoke detector in the restaurant.
   - ○ set on
   - ○ set off
   - ○ set out

4. Mr Bell <u>submitted</u> a new proposal to the director yesterday.
   - ○ put in
   - ○ put ahead
   - ○ put forward

Fill in the bubble next to the meaning of the phrasal verb in each sentence.

5. Why did you <u>turn down</u> such a good job offer?
   - ○ reduce
   - ○ fold
   - ○ reject

6. The athlete's attempt to break the world record nearly <u>came off</u>.
   - ○ removed
   - ○ succeeded
   - ○ fell

7. My grandfather's knee is <u>acting up</u> again and he has difficulty walking up the stairs.
   - ○ performing
   - ○ painful
   - ○ breaking

8. She tried to explain it to my brother, but he <u>brushed her off</u> impatiently.
   - ○ removed
   - ○ waved at her
   - ○ refused to listen

Revision

Underline the compound subjects or predicates in each sentence.

1. Jeff and I wandered along the empty streets.

2. We searched and ransacked the empty houses for food.

3. Tony and Jo came to look for us.

Combine the sentences below into one sentence that uses at least one appositive.

4. Their teacher is Mr Jin. He is the most well-liked teacher in the school.

   _____

5. Mr Tena is my uncle. He is a principal at a famous school.

   _____

Insert a comma or commas and underline the appositive in each sentence.

6. My teacher Mr Tey is a specialist in Mathematics and Science.

7. Fluffy our neighbor's dog liked to come over to our house.

8. Tim our classmate scored top marks in all his subjects.

Fill in the bubble next to the correct answer to complete each sentence.

9. _____ led to the downfall of many great men.
   ○ Greed   ○ Greedy   ○ Satisfaction

10. Whenever there is a big income divide, _____ breeds in society.
    ○ anger   ○ angry   ○ angrily

11. There was a great deal of _____ over the lack of communication.
   - ○ frustrating
   - ○ frustration
   - ○ hurting

12. She and her brother _____ to school every day.
   - ○ cycles
   - ○ cycle
   - ○ cycling

13. _____ is her passion; she sings everywhere she goes.
   - ○ Singing
   - ○ Sing
   - ○ Song

14. We _____ told to remain quiet until the guests left the room.
   - ○ were
   - ○ was
   - ○ had been

15. Celine, _____ mother is a celebrity, is a lonely and unhappy child.
   - ○ who
   - ○ whose
   - ○ whom

16. The lady standing over there is _____ mother.
   - ○ my
   - ○ mine
   - ○ me

17. I have my own toys and the boys have _____.
   - ○ their
   - ○ theirs
   - ○ them

Read each sentence. Form the correct gerund from the word in brackets.

18. _____ (race) is a high-risk sport.

19. Many racers have a passion for _____ (drive) and love the thrills of it.

20. _____ (train) is a necessity for all athletes and this includes racers.

21. _____ (sleep) is essential, as rest is very important.

114

Read each sentence. Write a pronoun on the line that can replace the underlined words.

22. <u>Movies</u> can make people laugh, cry and feel different emotions.

    _____

23. <u>The actor</u> really makes you empathize with him. _____

24. <u>My sister</u> wants to take up acting. _____

25. <u>My brother and I</u> think that she won't be any good at it. _____

26. <u>My father</u>, however, is supportive of her decision. _____

Circle the correct pronoun to complete each sentence.

27. She wanted (him / he) to help her.

28. Although the man was willing to, (he / him) did not have the ability to do so.

29. The man told (she / her) that there was nothing he could do.

30. Finally, (them / they) came to ask our family for help.

31. (We / Us) decided to do what we could and help raise the money the woman needed.

Change each sentence from direct to indirect speech and vice versa.

32. "I am giving you a handmade gift," the little girl said.

    _____

33. The children explained that they had gone for a swim.

    _____

Join the two sentences using a suitable relative pronoun.

34. The man's bicycle is being repaired. He is my uncle.

_____

35. The girl is missing. She is a student from my school.

_____

36. The props are in the dressing room. We made them for the school play.

_____

Fill in the bubble next to the correct quantifier to complete each sentence.

37. There are _____ opportunities for you, but you must learn to make use of those opportunities.
   ○ many   ○ much   ○ any

38. _____ of the time was taken up by school-council activities.
   ○ Many   ○ Much   ○ A few

39. Is there _____ milk left in the bottle?
   ○ many   ○ much   ○ any

40. There are only _____ pairs left, so you had better take them soon.
   ○ a few   ○ some   ○ much

Fill in the blanks with suitable modal verbs.

41. Camels _____ go for many days without water as they are able to store water in their bodies.

42. I _____ wake up early tomorrow so that I can get there early.

43. You _____ finish your antibiotics, otherwise you won't get well.

44. _____ you help to get that from the top shelf as I can't reach it?

45. I _____ spend a lot of time with my grandparents when I was young as my parents had to work.

46. When we were younger, my grandmother _____ bring us to the playground every day after school.

Fill in the bubble next to the adjective that correctly completes each sentence.

47. The talk was _____, and all of us were excited by the new findings.
   ○ fascinating   ○ fascinated   ○ fascinate

48. The latest news made history and we all felt _____ that a cure would be discovered.
   ○ hoping   ○ hopeful   ○ hope

49. We must keep this new technology out of the hands of _____ people who might abuse it.
   ○ greedy   ○ greed   ○ angry

Write the correct order of adjectives on the line.

50. (small, white, fluffy)   a _____ cat

51. (strong, Italian, young)   a _____ model

52. (pretty, pink, metal)   a _____ bicycle

Fill in the blanks with the correct form of the verb in brackets.

53. Professor Li _____ (study) the data for three hours when the phone rang.

54. The caller _____ (be) a strange man.

55. He _____ (identify) himself as Mr Park.

56. Mr Park claimed that he _____ (work) on some new technology the previous year that was related to her data.

57. He _____ (hope) to collaborate with her to develop a revolutionary biochip.

58. He asked if she _____ (develop) anything yet.

59. Professor Li _____ (be) not sure if she could trust him.

60. She _____ (spend) too much of her research budget and new sources of funds would be welcome.

61. Finally, she _____ (agree) to meet him for further discussions.

62. After some preliminary discussions, they decided that they _____ (collaborate) with each other.

63. Professor Li _____ (head) a new team of researchers to develop the biochip.

Fill in the bubble next to the adverb or intensifier that best completes each sentence.

64. I was _____ happy to find the precious ring that I had lost.
   ○ extremely   ○ rather   ○ barely

65. We could _____ hear her as she was speaking very softly.
   ○ somewhat   ○ really   ○ barely

66. The young boy jumped up and down _____ when he heard that he would get a new toy.
   ○ excited   ○ excitedly   ○ excitement

Fill in the bubble next to the connector that correctly completes the sentence.

67. You can choose the blue or the red dress, _____ you can't have both.
   ○ but   ○ because   ○ until

68. _____ I like the blue dress, I think it is too expensive.
   ○ Although   ○ Even   ○ However

69. I would have to save up quite a lot of money _____ I can buy the dress.
   ○ before   ○ after   ○ since

70. My parents decided to get it for me _____ they wanted to reward me for doing well in my studies.
   ○ until   ○ while   ○ because

Read each sentence. Fill in the blank with the correct form of the verb given in brackets.

71. If I had known this would happen, I _____ (allow) them to get married.

72. If it rains, they _____ (take) out their umbrellas.

73. If I knew her address, I _____ (deliver) the present myself.

Change the sentences from active voice to passive voice and vice versa.

74. The postman sent the package to the wrong address.

_____

75. The mystery was uncovered by the bounty hunters.

_____

Answer Key

Page 5

1. <u>Annemarie and Ellen</u> are good friends.
2. <u>Their homes and families</u> are in Denmark.
3. The girls sometimes <u>talk or giggle with Annemarie's sister</u>.
4. All three children <u>joke, laugh and play games together</u>.
5. <u>Families and friends</u> help each other in times of need.
6. During the war, the families <u>had to leave their homes and hide their belongings</u>.
7. Annemarie's family <u>hid Ellen and kept her safe</u>.
8. Ellen <u>read and sang to Annemarie's sister, Kirsti</u>.
9. <u>Ellen and Annemarie</u> played with Kirsti.
10. <u>Both the Rosens and the Johansens</u> survived the war.

Accept all reasonable answers.

Page 6

1. Families and friends help each other during times of hardship.
2. Many people survive the war with luck, intelligence and courage.
3. Families hid in the houses or fled to the forest.
4. Sometimes, families were torn apart or separated.
5. Many young people joined the army or worked in factories.
6. Many struggled to find food and drinking water.

Page 7

1. <u>George, Tina and I</u> are playground monitors.
2. We <u>watch for problems and solve them</u>.
3. <u>Keith and Tracy</u> asked me for help with a problem.
4. Their friend, Matt, <u>hit a ball and lost it on the school roof</u>.
5. <u>Tina and I</u> found Matt in a corner of the playground.
6. He <u>showed us where it went and asked if we could help retrieve it</u>.
7. Tina <u>looked up, turned and walked over to Miss Weiss</u>.
8. Miss Weiss <u>told us to find the custodian or find another ball</u>.
9. Matt smiled and went to find the custodian.
10. Miss Weiss and I waited for Matt to return.

Accept all reasonable answers.

Page 8

1. Bananas, <u>my favorite fruit</u>, are part of our dessert this evening.
2. The old lady in the red cardigan, <u>Mrs Briar</u>, lost her purse while shopping at the supermarket.
3. I have to renew my library book, <u>*Animal Farm*</u>, today to avoid late charges.
4. Our cousin, <u>Jayme</u>, will be representing her school in a fencing tournament next month.
5. Mr Cheung, <u>the man with a short beard</u>, helped the police arrest the thief.
6. Singapore is a multiracial and multicultural society.
7. Miss White is in the wash.
8. Daniel topped my class in Mathematics last year.

Page 9

1. The sun, a big ball of burning gas, is an important star in our solar system.
2. My sister is trying on a gorgeous wedding gown, the one with the beautiful beads, in the fitting room.
3. The mischievous boys from Class 6B, who had played a prank on their teacher, were punished severely by the principal.
4. I saw Josephine, my mom's secretary, take the stack of documents from the photocopier.
5. Gingerbread Man, one of Disney's characters, was giving out balloons to children during the parade.
6. Their eldest daughter, Rose, dislikes being named after a flower.
7. *The Sunflower*, a beautiful work of art, was painted by Vincent Van Gogh.
8. Peter's sister, Martha, has a new sling bag with a floral print.
9. Harry Potter, a powerful wizard, has a scar on his forehead.

Page 10

1. Bethany and Chris
2. Christmas
3. the younger of the twins
4. Mount Everest
5. lasagna with meatballs
6. A philanthropist, <u>Steven Smith,</u> donated a huge sum of money to help the victims of the tsunami.
7. Fluffy, <u>Grandma's cat,</u> loves to purr softly on her lap while she knits in her rocking chair.
8. On Christmas Day, we ate at Zappy, <u>our favorite restaurant</u>.

9. Tiffany, <u>the most polite student in the class</u>, won an award at the school assembly.
10. He was ecstatic when he received his birthday present, <u>a new mobile phone</u>.

Page 11
1. Underline: was ; Circle: car
2. Underline: is, wants ; Circle: everyone, nobody
3. Underline: has ; Circle: either of the parents
4. Underline: was ; Circle: bunch of bananas
5. Underline: is ; Circle: Hansel
6. is   7. belongs   8. patrols
9. was   10. is   11. dissolves
12. Does

Page 12
1. Underline: were, were ; Circle: cookies, they
2. Underline: keep ; Circle: Exercise and a balanced diet
3. Underline: were ; Circle: neither the pilot nor the passengers
4. Underline: are ; Circle: mom and dad
5. Underline: have taken ; Circle: We
6. Were   7. participates   8. have
9. scavenge   10. have   11. are
12. enjoy

Page 13
1. announce   2. has   3. helps   4. have
5. enjoys   6. wants   7. interests   8. are
9. am   10. make

Page 14
1. perseverance   2. chivalry
3. popularity   4. honesty, integrity
5. disappointment   6. greed, discontentment
7. unity   8. beauty
9. Hunger   10. vanity
11. Jealousy   12. emptiness

Page 15
1. happiness   2. creativity   3. action
4. agreement   5. freedom   6. difficulty
7. enjoyment   8. loneliness   9. poverty
10. sadness   11. truth   12. invention
13. Creativity   14. amazement   15. cruelty
16. happiness

Page 16
1. hardship   2. pride   3. slavery
4. precaution   5. negligence   6. admiration
7. justice   8. importance   9. danger
10. imagination

Page 17
1. Gardening   2. swimming, dancing
3. controlling their emotions
4. ringing of the phone   5. Visiting
6. chirping of the crickets   7. Smoking
8. writing, acting   9. lying
10. eating   11. Stealing   12. Sleeping

Page 18
1. jogging   2. traveling   3. Worrying
4. living   5. sharing   6. knitting
7. cooking   8. washing   9. cleaning
10. ironing   11. singing   12. reading
13. sleeping

Page 19
1. painting   2. smoking   3. Skiing
4. Crying   5. chatting   6. windsurfing
7. complaining   8. screaming   9. recycling
10. working

Page 20
1. they   2. we   3. she   4. we
5. it   7. they = people, it = book
8. We = Amy and Duncan, I = Amy
9. She = Emma, them = eggs
10. He, his = Timmy, them = shoes

Page 21
1. they   2. it   3. he   4. they
5. she   6. her   7. it   8. we
9. us   10. them   11. her
Accept all reasonable answers.

Page 22
1. them   2. they   3. She   4. her   5. him
6. we   7. it   8. us   9. me   10. I

Page 23
1. Underline: him ; Circle: neighbor
2. Underline: they ; Circle: roses
3. Underline: it ; Circle: garden
4. Underline: them ; Circle: holes
5. Underline: you ; Circle: woodcutter

6. The woodcutter's wife asked <u>him</u> to go to the woods.
                O
    S   O   S
7. "<u>I</u> want <u>you</u> to chop some wood," <u>she</u> said.
    S   O
8. "<u>We</u> have guests coming to visit <u>us</u>," said the woodcutter's wife.

121

9. "<u>They</u> will be here soon. Let's serve <u>them</u> dinner," <u>she</u> said.

   S   O

10. The woodcutter found an ax and <u>he</u> picked <u>it</u> up.

   S   O

11. "<u>I</u> will be back soon," the woodcutter told <u>her</u>.

Page 24
1. him   2. her   3. her
4. They   5. I   6. He
7. We   8. she   9. Her
10. He
Accept all reasonable answers.

Page 25
1. We   2. They   3. I
4. me   5. it   6. correct as is
7. them   8. Mark and me   9. She and I
10. He and I

Page 26
1. Circle: My, family   2. Circle: our, attic
3. Circle: their, honeymoon
4. Circle: her, bicycle   5. Circle: his, diary
6. Circle: its, key   7. Circle: your, house
8. my   9. your   10. his   11. her
12. its   13. our   14. their

Page 27
1. their   2. her   3. my
4. mine   5. her
6. Which dresses in the closet are hers?
7. This is their collection of dried flowers.
8. I am enjoying his book.
9. Her disappointment showed clearly.
10. Is this his idea?

Page 28
1. my   2. her   3. theirs
4. their   5. mine   6. Their
7. its   8. Her   9. his
10. hers

Page 29
1. who   2. whom   3. whose
4. that   5. who
6. Circle: who ; Underline: students
7. Circle: that ; Underline: shop
8. Circle: who ; Underline: children
9. Circle: whose ; Underline: man
10. Circle: which ; Underline: bus

11. Circle: who ; Underline: girl

Page 30
1. which   2. who   3. who
4. whom   5. whose
Accept all reasonable answers.

Page 31
1. that   2. which   3. whose
4. that   5. who
6. The adorable baby who is sleeping in the room is my niece.
7. The fisherman whose boat capsized due to the storm is safe.
8. These are the carnations that I bought for my mother's birthday.

Page 32
1. a lot of   2. Much   3. each
4. None   5. Many   6. some
7. any   8. a few   9. Most
10. Every   11. some   12. All

Page 33
1. √   2. X   3. X
4. √   5. √   6. X
7. little   8. many   9. any
10. a lot of   11. some   12. much

Page 34
1. plenty   2. many   3. little
4. number   5. many   6. much
7. Few   8. many   9. lots of
10. a little

Page 35
1. go   2. accompany 3. buy
4. walk   5. run   6. stay
7. ride   8. sing   9. rain
10. escape   11. decorate

Page 36
1. watch   2. tidy   3. leave
4. succeed   5. see   6. sell
Accept all reasonable answers.

Page 37
1. dash   2. stop   3. raise
4. put   5. change
Accept all reasonable answers.

Page 38
1. may   2. can   3. could
4. can   5. must   6. may

7. could 8. might 9. may
10. can 11. may

Page 39
1. should 2. ought to 3. shall
4. must 5. will 6. shall
7. will 8. should / ought to / must
9. will 10. should / ought to / must
11. should / ought to
12. should / ought to / must

Page 40
1. may 2. shall 3. must
4. should 5. can 6. can (A)
7. will (I) 8. must (O) 9. could (A)
10. must (O)

Page 41
1. need (N) 2. dared (B) 3. dare (O)
4. need (N) 5. dared (B) 6. need
7. dared 8. need 9. Need
10. dare

Page 42
1. should / ought to 2. Could / Can
3. might / may 4. dare
5. would 6. should / ought to
Accept all reasonable answers.

Page 43
1. might 2. can 3. need
4. dare 5. dare 6. should
7. dare 8. need 9. will
10. can

Page 44
1. will (present) 2. used to (past)
3. would (past) 4. will (present)
5. used to (past) 6. used to 7. used to
8. would 9. would 10. used to
11. would

Page 45
1. will 2. will 3. will
4. used to 5. used to 6. would
7. will
Accept all reasonable answers.

Page 46
1. would 2. will 3. would
4. used to 5. used to 6. can
7. would 8. should 9. will
10. must

Page 47
1. hungry, black, sausage 2. friendly, short
3. horror 4. responsible
5. beautiful, colorful, glass 6. quickest
7. gingerbread, adorable, delicious
8. oldest, active 9. straight
10. unexpected 11. difficult
12. new 13. interesting

Page 48
1. teachable 2. courageous 3. faithful
4. adorable 5. boring 6. attractive
7. helpful 8. interesting 9. famous
10. exciting
Accept all reasonable answers.

Page 49
1. expensive 2. independent 3. invaluable
4. fierce 5. steep 6. greedy
7. worried 8. painful 9. kind
10. bitter

Page 50
1. Underline: proud, Chinese ; Circle: man
2. Underline: pretty, porcelain ; Circle: tea set
3. Underline: flowery, red, wrapping ; Circle: paper
4. Underline: skinny, young ; Circle: lady
5. Underline: soft, blue, Oriental ; Circle: pillow

Adjectives							
Opinion	Size	Age	Shape	Color	Origin	Material	Purpose
silly	gigantic	young	triangular	blue	chinese	cotton	sleeping
useful	tiny	old	round	yellow	African	metal	
strong	tall			brown	American	plastic	

Page 51
1. an old plastic table
2. a beautiful white colonial house
3. a pretty glass serving bowl
4. a cute tiny brown mongrel
5. pink cotton socks
6. short, yellow 7. boring, old, History
8. amazing new 9. comfortable, old leather
10. intelligent, young

Page 52
1. ugly big black 2. scary long pointed
3. excellent dairy 4. round white recyclable
5. empty glass 6. tiny round reading
7. popular slim German
8. fragile, pink porcelain flower
9. tall eccentric Science
10. mysterious old haunted

Page 53

1. full of horror
2. in the album
3. next to the cottage
4. in the attic
5. in this special zoo
6. (√) Grandma used to live in a house built of wood.
7. (√) The baby in the stroller is crying furiously because he is cold and wet.
8. (√) My great grand uncle was a man of great wealth; he owned acres of land.
9. (√) Tigers with white fur tend to be bigger at birth.
10. (√) Mr Hyde led a life of decadence.

Page 54

1. The girl in detention class is mischievous.
2. The box under the bed is covered with cobwebs.
3. The lawn between the two old houses is full of tall weeds.
4. The cat with the veterinarian is our pet cat Dolly.
5. Did you see the man leaving the car park?

Accept all reasonable answers.

Page 55

1. (√) The shoes in the yard are muddy.
2. (√) The man lurking outside our house had a black umbrella.
3. (√) The ambulance behind our bus is sounding the siren.
4. (√) The man in the hammock is having a nap.
5. (√) The empty land beside our house will be turned into a park soon.
6. The motorcycle in the garage belongs to Uncle Vincent.
7. The beautiful actress on the stage looks familiar.
8. The pot on the table is made of earth.
9. The people on strike work in the airline industry.

Page 56

1. felt
2. decided, tasted
3. seemed
4. was
5. looked
6. (√) The curry chicken tasted spicy.
7. (√) He grew tired of waiting for his turn to play on the slide.
8. (√) She looked fine even though she had not slept for three nights.
9. (√) The music sounded so soothing that before long, the children were fast asleep.
10. (√) He felt disappointed that he could not go to Disneyland.

Page 57

1. looked
2. were
3. feel
4. is
5. appeared
6. seemed
7. felt
8. appeared
9. is, is
10. saved
11. smells
12. feels

Page 58

1. thought
2. smelled
3. appeared
4. seemed
5. were
6. Underline: was ; Circle: Alice
7. Underline: seemed ; Circle: She
8. Underline: felt ; Circle: she
9. Underline: looked, thought ; Circle: She, we
10. Underline: were ; Circle: We

Page 59

1. barked, approached
2. are planning
3. cries
4. has been waiting
5. had taken
6. were patrolling
7. brought
8. was crying
9. has been worrying
10. will get
11. feels

Page 60

Accept all reasonable answers.

Page 61

1. sleeps
2. will dance
3. was playing
4. will be leaving
5. ran
6. had been keeping
7. sang
8. are living
9. has been helping
10. were trying

Page 62

1. past
2. present
3. past
4. past
5. past
6. stolen
7. sprained
8. boiling
9. forbidden
10. tiring
11. smoked, roasted

Page 63

1. crying
2. worried
3. shown
4. waiting
5. hidden
6. drunk
7. Having tied
8. spoilt
9. had fallen
10. Having slept

Accept all reasonable answers.

Page 64

1. have confused
2. torn
3. given
4. have got
5. broken
6. Taking
7. waiting
8. written

Page 65

1. had lost
2. had seen
3. had not booked
4. had left
5. had dumped
6. had arranged
7. X
8. X
9. had cleared
10. X
11. had expected

124

Page 66

1. Underline: Mum had discarded all his favorite car magazines ; Circle: Dad looked grumpy
2. Underline: After the students had done the experiment ; Circle: they wrote a report on it
3. Underline: the customers had lined up outside this restaurant ; Circle: it opened for business
4. Underline: the players waited ; Circle: the referee blew the whistle
5. Underline: we had not locked one of our windows properly ; Circle: a thief successfully broke into our house
6. After 7. after 8. Before

Accept all reasonable answers.

Page 67

1. had made 2. arrived 3. went
4. had noticed 5. began 6. had lived
7. has migrated 8. received

Page 68

1. had ... been paying 2. had been losing
3. had been raining 4. had been having
5. had ... been eating 6. had been weeping
7. had been painting 8. had been exercising
9. had been screaming 10. had not been preparing
11. had been riding 12. had been lying

Page 69

1. waited ; Rachel had been waiting at the bus stop for two hours before it came.
2. looked ;The children had been looking forward to seeing her all week.
3. cared ; Michelle had been caring for them the past week as Rachel was busy.
4. stood ; The children had been standing at the doorway for a long time.
5. hoped ; They had been hoping to show her all the things they did during the week.

Accept all reasonable answers.

Page 70

1. had been learning 2. had been teaching
3. had been cooking 4. was crying
5. had been jogging 6. has been cleaning
7. had been cycling 8. slept
9. have been writing

Page 71

1. am going to watch 2. will be
3. is starting 4. will be leaving
5. will be finishing 6. is going to travel
7. will shut 8. is going to apply

9. will be lying 10. are having
11. is staying

Page 72

Accept all reasonable answers for Questions 1–4.
5. will sell 6. am going 7. is working
8. will be meeting 9. will stay / will be staying
10. will attend / will be attending

Page 73

1. will be working 2. mailed
3. are going to celebrate 4. am taking
5. will be performing 6. will discuss
7. met 8. will take

Page 74

1. am getting (PC) 2. wakes (PS)
3. is raining (PC) 4. has landed (PP)
5. has been ringing (PPC) 6. have cleaned (PP)
7. had been swimming (PastPC)
8. had looked (PastP) 9. bought (PastS)
10. had been worrying (PastPC)
11. was flashing (PastC) 12. had blown (PastP)

Page 75

1. present 2. future 3. future
4. present 5. future 6. present
7. were arguing 8. had been watching
9. was going to stop, was smoking
10. arrived 11. bought, uses

Page 76

1. past continuous 2. present perfect
3. present perfect continuous
4. past perfect continuous
5. am working 6. has been
7. plays 8. was having
9. had completed

Page 77

1. angrily 2. almost 3. slowly
4. probably 5. usually 6. well
7. walked 8. decorated 9. blue
10. talented 11. hot 12. old, walks

Page 78

1. gracefully 2. terribly 3. finally
4. early 5. past 6. immediately
7. badly 8. successfully 9. loudly
10. slightly 11. firmly

Page 79

1. eventually 2. wearily 3. recently
4. definitely 5. certainly 6. suddenly
7. accidentally 8. delightfully 9. hungrily

Page 80
1. extremely
2. absolutely
3. totally
4. barely
5. really
6. rather
7. quite
8. a bit
9. very
10. quite
11. very
12. quite

Page 81
1. Circle: extremely ; Underline: angry
2. Circle: quite ; Underline: quickly
3. Circle: too ; Underline: hard
4. Circle: slightly ; Underline: different
5. Circle: enough ; Underline: experienced
6. That radio is a bit loud.
7. The team did the job fairly quickly.
8. This dress is not big enough.
9. I feel a lot better now.
10. This drawing is almost perfect.

Page 82
1. almost
2. very
3. completely
4. so
5. really
6. very
7. totally
8. quite

Page 83
1. despite
2. but
3. or
4. although
5. nevertheless
6. because
7. although
8. but
9. but
10. unless
11. or
12. whereas

Page 84
1. Ernest wants to eat at home, but his wife wants to dine out.
2. Our receptionist answers phone calls and greets customers.
3. Annie said nothing because she was too angry to speak.
4. while
5. as soon as
6. until
7. before
8. when
9. since

Page 85
1. whereas
2. until
3. while
4. but
5. unless
6. although
7. despite
8. because

Page 86
1. I want to go to the movies, but my friend Pat does not.
2. It rained last night, and we had to stay home.
3. Ed will drive to Texas, or he will take the train.
4. It snowed this morning, but the sun came out in the afternoon.
5. We wanted to ride our bikes home, but mine had a flat tire.
6. The whistle blew and the train pulled out of the station.
7. I will finish the job today or Bob will finish it tomorrow.

Page 87
1. Our cousins arrived, and we were very happy to see them.
2. Eileen had cut her hair short, but her twin sister Emily still had long hair.
3. They had always looked exactly alike, and I could not get used to them.
4. Would they play with me or only with my older sisters?
5. Eileen and Emily gave me a hug.
6. Our parents went into the kitchen to talk, but the rest of us preferred to be outside.
7. At dinner, Mom said the twins could stay with us or we could go stay with them.

Page 88
1. correct as is
2. correct as is
3. bookshelf, but I
4. correct as is
5. correct as is
6. but
7. but
8. or
9. and
10. but

Page 89
Underline sentences 1, 3, 5.
7. The teacher returned the homework
8. The students are busy studying
9. John and Maria went out to watch a movie
10. You have to wait
11. I must get to the post office

Page 90
1. until
2. when
3. because
4. if
5. <u>Aesop wrote a story about a shepherd boy</u> <u>who was protecting a flock of sheep from a wolf</u>.
6. <u>The students left the playground early</u> <u>because it started to rain</u>.
7. <u>The cat licked her paws</u> <u>after she had played with the yarn</u>.
8. <u>Fighting infection was difficult</u> <u>until penicillin was discovered</u>.
9. <u>Grandma gave her house key to me to keep</u> <u>because she trusted me</u>.
10. <u>The Great Barrier Reef is the world's largest reef</u> <u>which contains an abundance of marine life</u>.
Accept all reasonable answers.

Page 91
1. dependent clause
2. independent clause
3. independent clause
4. independent clause
5. dependent clause
6. who
7. which
8. that
9. where
10. when

Page 92
1. third
2. second
3. second

126

4. third 5. first 6. first
7. first 8. third

Page 93

1. If you win the game, I will buy you lunch.
2. If I went to bed earlier, I would have difficulty falling asleep.
3. If you had come to the theme park with us, we would have had a ride on the roller coaster.
4. If you brought your camera, you could take a photo.
5. If you had watched the movie, you might have enjoyed it.
6. If I find Connie's address, I will send her an invitation to my party.
7. If you had swallowed the washing detergent, it would have killed you.
8. If my brother had a dictionary, he would check the meaning of the word.
9. If Kim had come to school today, I would have lent her my book.
10. If I forget my best friend's birthday, she will feel upset and disappointed.
11. If my back aches tomorrow, I will stay at home.

Page 94

1. third 2. first 3. third
4. second 5. first 6. could have given
7. breaks 8. came 9. proposes

Page 95

1. Elvin (is) (chewing gum).
2. The tower (is) (tall).
3. I (am eating).
4. My leg (has) (a big wound).
5. My teacher (told) (a story).
6. The turtle (is) (laying eggs).
7. object 8. verb 9. subject
10. object 11. verb

Page 96

1. b,e 2. a, d 3. c
4. Molly looks pale.
5. We are having a great time.
6. Daniel had an accident.
7. The children are eating ice cream.

Page 97

1. object 2. complement 3. object
4. verb 5. subject + verb + object
6. subject + verb + complement
7. subject + verb
8. subject + verb + complement

Page 98

1. on the porch 2. loudly
3. with a smile 4. at the grocery store
5. accidentally 6. in a taxi 7. verb
8. object 9. object 10. adverbial
11. subject 10. adverbial

Page 99

1. b,d 2. a, c, e, f
3. Mom will buy a teddy bear.
4. Connie's house is nearby.
5. The eagle is flying in the sky.
Accept all reasonable answers.

Page 100

1. direct object 2. verb
3. adverbial 4. subject
5. The couple was celebrating their wedding anniversary at the restaurant.
6. We gave the couple a special cake.
7. The man gave the lady a bouquet of flowers.
8. She bought him a tie.

Page 101

1. active 2. active 3. passive
4. active 5. passive 6. active
7. Mom 8. Christine 9. we
10. Leonardo da Vinci 11. The thief
12. the sponsors

Page 102

1. The house was decorated for Christmas by us.
2. The invites were sent out for the party by Cheryl.
3. The delicious spread was cooked by my parents.
4. The beautiful flowers were brought by my cousins.
5. Various charitable organizations organized the event.
6. A panel of experts discussed the topics.
7. Each group presented different solutions.
8. Various groups held protests outside the venue.

Page 103

1. James 2. manager 3. applicants
4. applicants
5. The firefighters rescued the villagers from the fire.
6. A teenager was suspected of committing arson.
7. The suspect was caught after four months.
8. A reporter reported the incident in the news.
9. The villagers' homes were rebuilt after many months.

Page 104

1. direct 2. direct 3. indirect
4. indirect 5. the day before
6. went 7. asked
8. she had been friendly

Page 105

1. Alex said that he was busy fixing the bookshelf.
2. Leo said, "I have been studying Spanish for one year."
3. My sister said that Mom had cleaned the windows already.
4. Dan said that he was meeting his friend at the station the next day.
5. the previous week
6. the previous week
7. she, she could pass her test
8. him

Page 106

1. Jane said that she was having tea with May.
2. Joe said that Tom had sent a postcard to him.
3. "I have passed my Math examination," said Kim.
4. "We want to get married," said the couple.
5. Paul said that he had forgotten to close the windows.
6. Janice asked if I could help her buy movie tickets.
7. Justin said that he would do it the next day.

Page 107

1. on the counter
2. below the table
3. Above the cabinet
4. in the silver pan
5. into the room
6. to
7. for
8. to
9. down
10. on
11. across
12. in

Page 108

1. under
2. through
3. above
4. into
5. in, for
6. behind, around
7. X, on
8. X, on
9. X
10. on
11. in, in, at

Page 109

1. below
2. for
3. off
4. between
5. under, on
6. on, down
7. to, across

Page 110

1. Circle: took ; Underline: off
2. Circle: carry ; Underline: on
3. Circle: blasted ; Underline: off
4. Circle: keep ; Underline: up
5. Circle: closed ; Underline: down
6. Circle: carved ; Underline: out
7. on
8. to
9. down
10. out
11. off

Page 111

1. put off
2. looking into
3. send out
4. fall out
5. cut in
6. set up
7. started crying
8. stopped working
9. hit hard and opened
10. failed

Page 112

1. call off
2. pull down
3. set off
4. put in
5. reject
6. succeeded
7. painful
8. refused to listen

Pages 113–120

1. Jeff and I
2. searched and ransacked the empty houses for food
3. Tony and Jo
4. Their teacher, Mr Jin, is the most well-liked teacher in the school.
5. Mr Tena, my uncle, is a principal at a famous school.
6. My teacher, <u>Mr Tey</u>, is a specialist in Mathematics and Science.
7. Fluffly, <u>our neighbor's dog</u>, liked to come over to our house.
8. Tim, <u>our classmate</u>, scored top marks in all his subjects.
9. Greed
10. anger
11. frustration
12. cycle
13. Singing
14. were
15. whose
16. my
17. theirs
18. Racing
19. driving
20. Training
21. Sleeping
22. They
23. He
24. She
25. We
26. He
27. him
28. he
29. her
30. they
31. We
32. The little girl said that she was giving me a handmade gift.
33. "We went for a swim," the children explained.
34. The man whose bicycle is being repaired is my uncle.
35. The girl who is missing is a student from my school.
36. The props that we made for the school play are in the dressing room.
37. many
38. Much
39. any
40. a few
41. can
42. will
43. must
44. Can / Could
45. used to
46. would
47. fascinating
48. hopeful
49. greedy
50. small, white, fluffy
51. strong, young Italian
52. pretty pink metal
53. had been studying
54. was
55. identified
56. had worked
57. hopes
58. has developed
59. was
60. has spent
61. agreed
62. would collaborate
63. will head
64. extremely
65. barely
66. excitedly
67. but
68. Although
69. before
70. because
71. would have allowed
72. will take
73. would deliver
74. The package was sent to the wrong address.
75. The bounty hunters uncovered the mystery.